Magnificent Meditations

of

Assurance
Peace
and
Wisdom

From the Bible
With comparative topic references
between Old and New Testaments

Compiled and annotated by
Dr. Armen Mesrobian

MAGNIFICENT MEDITATIONS OF ASSURANCE PEACE AND WISDOM
Compiled and annotated by
Dr. Armen Z. Mesrobian
Professor Emeritus, University Of Illinois

Copyright © 1998 by Armen Z. Mesrobian.
All rights reserved. No part of this book may be
reproduced, stored or transmitted in any form
or by any means without prior written
permission of the publisher.

Library of Congress Catalog Card Number:
97-95009

International Standard Book Number:
ISBN 0-9632735-2-3

E-mail: EPS EXC PS
FAX: 847-251-1582

Printed in the United States of America

E P S EXCEL PUBLISHING SERVICES
P.O. Box 86   Wilmette, Illinois 60091

An Invitation To Fill Your Needs

Do you have hurts, sorrows, hungers, thirsts, unmet needs, aspirations and hopes? Then seek the fulfilling words of God for your answers. Look in the Topical Contents pages for guidance.

....

Ask, and it shall be given you; seek, and ye shall find; knock, and it shall be opened unto you. (Luke 11:9)

Dedication

To the One without Whom
nothing would be possible,
and with Whom everything is possible,

Acknowledgments

I am deeply grateful to all that have spread and handed down to us from the earliest times, the Word of God, the Holy Scriptures, our Sacred Inheritance.

Preface

The journey into meditation and faith need not be a lonely one. Believe in the Lord, and He shall be with you always and guide your way. With repeated reading and meditation, even the more difficult verses will become clear to you. He will enlighten you.

The selected verses of Scripture are from the King James Version of the Bible. Readers are encouraged to also consult the other versions of the Bible.

The writer or publisher are not responsible for any errors, typographical or other, that may have been inadvertently included.

The contents of this book are informational. Those who have serious meditative or spiritual problems should consult their own religious advisor.

••••••

Religious institutions, book stores and others wishing to make quantity purchases of this book are offered discounts and are invited to contact the publisher:

E P S EXCEL PUBLISHING SERVICES
1729 Forest Avenue
Wilmette, Illinois 60091
847-251-1582

Introduction

This collection of Bible verses is presented in response to the need for a fairly comprehensive reference of biblical passages of assurance, peace and wisdom for meditation. It is not a substitute for the entire Bible, which has many other features.

The enclosed selections contain wise answers for the deepest yearnings of our hearts. It has a convenient size for carrying on one's person, as a sacred Companion, for frequent reading, study and prayer.

May these inspirational words of love and peace encourage you to build a strong faith. Let us meditate on the Word of the Lord and serve Him and our fellow men, always.

Prayerfully,
Armen Mesrobian

The Bible

The word Bible is derived from the Greek word biblia, meaning "books", and contains the sacred writings of Judaism and Christianity. The Bible has two parts. The Old Testament, consists of the Holy Scriptures of the Jewish people. The New Testament, records the story of Jesus and the beginnings of Christianity.

The Bible has been translated into almost 1,600 languages and is by far the most widely distributed book in the world.

Jesus Healing the Deaf, Blind Man
By Gustave Doré
The Doré Bible Illustrations, Dover Publications, Inc.

Illustrations

New Testament Selections

Jesus Healing the Deaf, Blind Man	8
The Nativity of Jesus	39
The Baptism of Jesus	48
The Good Samaritan	87
Jesus Blessing the Bread and Wine	98
The Holy Scriptures with Cross	103
Jesus Carrying His Cross	123
The Sermon on the Mount	145
The Last Supper	181
The Holy Bible	189

Moses Presenting The Ten Commandments
By Gustave Doré
The Doré Bible Illustrations, Dover Publications, Inc.

Illustrations

Old Testament Selections

Moses with the Ten Commandments	**10**
Torah Scrolls	**194**
The Star of David	**202**
The Menorah	**214**
Blowing the Shofar	**230**

Contents

Invitation To Fill Your Needs	3
Introduction	6
The Meaning Of The Bible	7
Illustrations List	9, 11

New Testament Section

Significance Of New Testament	16
The Lord's Prayer	17, 18
Topical Contents And Index	19
New Testament Verses	31
Epilogue	190

Old Testament Section

Significance Of Old Testament	195
Ten Commandments	197, 198
Topical Contents And Index	199
Psalms	203
Proverbs	225
Epilogue	235

Use the Topical Contents and Index on pages 19-29 and 199-202 as your guide through this book of meditation.

In certain passages the English of the King James Version may be confusing to some readers. In such verses, alternative modern usage words, in brackets, have been respectfully added to the original text.

New Testament Section

New Testament

The New Testament records the teachings and experiences of Jesus and the beginnings of Christianity and the early church. Its influence on history and culture is beyond measure.

Jesus Christ is the central subject of the New Testament. The paramount matter is the nature of Jesus as Christ, the Messiah or the Anointed one, Son of God and Lord. His divinity was declared. The second great importance is the Resurrection. The Messiah now came to signify, a self-sacrificing, crucified and risen Savior with a unique relationship to God.

Jesus declared the coming kingdom of God and practiced a ministry of love embodied in instruction, forgiveness of sin, and healing.

Lord's Prayer

The Lord's Prayer, the Our Father or Pater Noster, is the only form or manner of prayer assigned to his followers by Jesus Christ. This prayer appears in Matthew 6:9-13 and in Luke 11:2-4. In Matthew (the longer version) the prayer consists of invoking Our Father followed by seven requests, the first three asking for God's glorification, the last four seeking God's help and guidance. This great prayer is the main prayer and a binding influence of Christians.

The Lord's Prayer

After this manner therefore pray ye:

Our Father which art in heaven, Hallowed be thy name. Thy kingdom come. Thy will be done in earth, as it is in heaven.
Give us this day our daily bread.
And forgive us our debts, as we forgive our debtors.
And lead us not into temptation, but deliver us from evil: For thine is the kingdom, and the power, and the glory, for ever. Amen.

(Matthew 6:13)

Topical Contents
And Index
New Testament Section

Abide In Christ	31
Ability Through Christ	31
Abundance	31
All Things With God	32
Angels	33
Anger (Dealing With)	33
Ask	34
Author Of Our Faith	34
Author Of Peace	35
Author Of Our Salvation	35
Baptism	35
Beginning A New	36
Begotten Son	36
Believing In God	36
Birth Of Jesus	37

Blessed Be God	40
Blood Of Jesus	40
Born Again	42
Bread Alone	43
Brotherly Love	43
Calling Upon The Lord	44
Charity	44
Chastisement	46
Children	46
Christ	47
Christ Died For Us	49
Christ Oriented	49
Christ's Followers	50
Comfort	50
Commandments, Great	51
Commandments, Ten	52
Commands Of Jesus	52
Commitment To Christ	53

Condemnation, Handling It	54
Confession	55
Contentment	56
Contrition	57
Courage	59
Covetousness	59
Crown Of Righteousness	60
Death	60
Deliver Me From Evil	61
Denial Of Self	62
Despair, Conquering It	62
Doers Of The Word	63
Doing God's Work	63
Eat	64
Effective Prayer	64
End (The Last Days)	66
Enemies	67
Entertaining Strangers	68
Envy	68

Escape Condemnation	68
Eternal Life	69
Evil	70
Faith	70
Fear	72
Fellowship Of Believers	73
First And Last, **Alpha & Omega**	74
Fishers Of Men	74
Follow Me	75
Forbearance	75
Forgiveness	76
Freedom From Sin	77
Freedom In Christ	77
Fruitfulness	78
Fruit Of The Spirit	79
Gifts Of God	79
Glorify God	80

Glory Of God	80
God Is One	81
God Seeking	81
God's Gifts To Us	82
God's Help In Trouble	83
God's Love For Us	83
God's Personality	84
God's Power	85
Golden Rule	86
Good, All Things For	86
Good Samaritan	88
Grace	89
Guidance	89
Guilt	90
Harmony	90
Healing And Health	91
Help From God	92
Helping Others	92

Holy Spirit	93
Honesty	94
Hope	95
Hospitality	96
Humility	97
Hunger	97
Husbands And Wives	99
Inspiration From God	101
Jealousy	101
Jesus	102
Joy	104
Judge Not	104
Judgment Seat	105
Kingdom Of God	106
Kingship Of God	106
Laborers With God	107
Laziness	107
Life Everlasting	108
Live	109

Loneliness	109
Long Life	110
Lord's Prayer	17, 18, 157
Love	110
Love Of God For Us	111
Loving God	112
Lust	113
Lying	114
Man, What Is Man	114
Mansions, Father's House	114
Marriage	115
Mary	116
Meekness	118
Mercy	118
Mind Of God	119
Money	119
Mustard Seed	120
Near To God	121

Obedience To God	122
Old Age	124
Overcoming The World	125
Patience	125
Peace	126
Persecution	127
Pleasing God	127
Poverty	128
Power Of God	128
Praising God	129
Prayer, Lord's	17, 18, 130
Pride	131
Prodigal Son	132
Promises Of The Bible	134
Prosperity	135
Protection	135
Receiving What You Ask	136
Repentance	137
Rest	137

Resurrection	138
Revenge	138
Revival	138
Reward For Righteousness	139
Rich Man	140
Sadness	140
Salvation	141
Samaritan, Good	144
Seeking God	81, 145
Self Denial	65
Self-Worth	144
Sermon On The Mount	144
Serving God	167
Serving Others	167
Shame	168
Sickness	168
Signs Of The End	169
Sin	169
Soul	170

Sower	171
Speaking Badly (Maliciously)	172
Spirit, Fruit Of	173
Spirit Of Truth	173
Spirituality	173
Spiritual Health	173
Spiritual Trials	174
Strangers	174
Strength	175
Stress, Coping With It	175
Suffering	177
Tears Wiped Away	179
Temptation	180
The Last Supper	181
Thirst	182
Tidings Of Great Joy	182
Trinity, Holy	182
Trouble	83, 182

Trust In God	183
Understanding	184
Vengeance	184
Wait On The Lord	185
Walk In The Light	185
Wisdom	186
Witness	186
Word Of God	188
Worldliness	189
Epilogue New Testament	190

Notes

Abide In Christ

Draw nigh to God, and he will draw nigh to you. Cleanse your hands, ye sinners; and purify your hearts, ye double minded.   (James 4:8)

Ability Through Christ

I can do all things through Christ which strengtheneth me.
(Philippians 4:13)

Abundance

If ye abide in me, and my words abide in you, ye shall ask what ye will, and it shall be done unto you.
(John 15:7)

All Things With God

Jesus beheld them, and said unto them, with God all things are possible. (Matthew 19:26)

Jesus said unto him, If thou canst believe, all things are possible to him that believeth. (Mark 9:23)

And he said, Abba, Father, all things are possible unto thee; take away this cup from me: nevertheless not what I will, but what thou wilt.
(Mark 14:36)

With God All Things Are Possible.

Angels

Be not forgetful to entertain strangers: for thereby some have entertained angels unawares. (Hebrews 13:2)

Anger

But I say unto you, That whosoever is angry with his brother without a cause shall be in danger of the judgment: and whosoever shall say to his brother, Raca (idiot), shall be in danger of the council: but whosoever shall say, Thou fool, shall be in danger of hell fire. (Matthew 5:22)

Dearly beloved, avenge not yourselves, but rather give place unto wrath: for it is written, Vengeance is mine; I will repay, saith the Lord.
(Romans 12:19)

Ask

Whatsoever ye shall ask in my name, that will I do, that the Father may be glorified in the Son.

If ye shall ask any thing in my name, I will do it. (John 14:13-14)

Author Of Our Faith

Looking unto Jesus the author and finisher of our faith; who for the joy that was set before him endured the cross, despising the shame, and is set down at the right hand of the throne of God. (Hebrews 12:2)

If Ye Shall Ask Any Thing In My Name, I Will Do It.

Author Of Peace

God is not the author of confusion, but of peace, as in all churches of the saints. (1 Corinthians 14:33)

Author Of Our Salvation

Being made perfect, he became the author of eternal salvation unto all them that obey him; (Hebrews 5:9)

Baptism

John truly baptized with water; but ye shall be baptized with the Holy Ghost not many days hence. (Acts 1:5)

Beginning A New

If any man be in Christ, he is a new creature: old things are passed away; behold, all things are become new. (2 Corinthians 5:17)

Begotten Son, (Only)

God so loved the world, that he gave his only begotten Son, that whosoever believeth in him should not perish, but have everlasting life. (John 3:16)

Believing In God

As many as received him, to them gave he power to become the sons of God, even to them that believe on his name: (John 1:12)

Birth Of Jesus

Jacob begat Joseph the husband of Mary, of whom was born Jesus, who is called Christ.

Now the birth of Jesus Christ was on this wise: When as his mother Mary was espoused to Joseph, before they came together, she was found with child of the Holy Ghost.

Then Joseph her husband, being a just man, and not willing to make her a public example, was minded to put her away privily (secretly).

But while he thought on these things, behold, the angel of the Lord appeared unto him in a dream, saying, Joseph, thou son of David, fear not to take unto thee Mary thy wife: for that which is conceived in her is of the Holy Ghost.

And she shall bring forth a son, and thou shalt call his name Jesus: for he shall save his people from their sins. (Matthew 1:16,18-21)

Now when Jesus was born in Bethlehem of Judaea in the days of Herod the king, behold, there came wise men from the east to Jerusalem,

And, lo, the star, which they saw in the east, went before them, till it came and stood over where the young child was.

When they saw the star, they rejoiced with exceeding great joy.

And when they were come into the house, they saw the young child with Mary his mother, and fell down, and worshipped him: and when they had opened their treasures, they presented unto him gifts; gold, and frankincense, and myrrh. (Matthew 2:1, 9-11)

The Nativity Of Jesus
By Gustave Doré
The Doré Bible Illustrations, Dover Publications, Inc.

Blessed Be God

Blessed be the God and Father of our Lord Jesus Christ, which according to his abundant mercy hath begotten us again unto a lively hope by the resurrection of Jesus Christ from the dead, (1 Peter 1:3)

Blood Of Jesus

We, being (are) justified freely by his grace through the redemption that is in Christ Jesus:

Whom God hath set forth to be a propitiation (conciliation) through faith in his blood, to declare his righteousness for the remission of sins that are past, through the forbearance of God; (Romans 3:24-25)

Much more then, being now justified by his blood, we shall be saved from wrath through him. (Romans 5:9)

John to the seven churches which are in Asia: Grace be unto you, and peace, from him which is, and which was, and which is to come;...

And from Jesus Christ, who is the faithful witness, and the first begotten of the dead, and the prince of the kings of the earth. Unto him that loved us, and washed us from our sins in his own blood, (Revelation 1:4-5)

These are they which came out of great tribulation, and have washed their robes, and made them white in the blood of the Lamb. (Revelation 7:14)

Being Justified (Cleansed) By His Blood, We Shall Be Saved.

Born Again

He that findeth his life shall lose it: and he that loseth his life for my sake shall find it. (Matthew 10:39)

If any man be in Christ, he is a new creature: old things are passed away; behold, all things are become new. (2 Corinthians 5:17)

Being born again, not of corruptible seed, but of incorruptible, by the word of God, which liveth and abideth for ever. (1 Peter 1:23)

Jesus said, Verily, verily, I say unto thee, Except a man be born again, he cannot see the kingdom of God. (John 3:3)

Bread Alone, Not by

Man shall not live by bread alone, but by every word that proceedeth out of the mouth of God. (Matthew 4:4)

Brotherly Love

We know that we have passed from death unto life, because we love the brethren. He that loveth not his brother abideth in death. (1 John 3:14)

Be ye doers of the word, and not hearers only, deceiving your own selves. (James 1:22)

And the King shall answer and say unto them, Verily I say unto you, Inasmuch as ye have done it unto one of the least of these my brethren, ye have done it unto me. (Matthew 25:40)

Calling Upon The Lord

Not every one that saith unto me, Lord, Lord, shall enter into the kingdom of heaven; but he that doeth the will of my Father which is in heaven. (Matthew 7:21)

Verily, verily, I say unto you, He that heareth my word, and believeth on him that sent me, hath everlasting life, and shall not come into condemnation; but is passed from death unto life. (John 5:24)

Charity

Now abideth faith, hope, charity, these three; but the greatest of these is charity (love). (1 Corinthians 13:13)

Take heed that ye do not your alms before men, to be seen of them: otherwise ye have no reward of your Father which is in heaven.

That thine alms may be in secret: and thy Father which seeth in secret himself shall reward thee openly.
(Matthew 6:1,4)

Whosoever shall give you a cup of water to drink in my name, because ye belong to Christ, verily I say unto you, he shall not lose his reward.
(Mark 9:41)

I have showed you all things, how that so labouring ye ought to support the weak, and to remember the words of the Lord Jesus, how he said, It is more blessed to give than to receive.
(Acts 20:35)

Chastisement

Whom the Lord loveth he chasteneth, and scourgeth every son whom he receiveth.

If ye endure chastening, God dealeth with you as with sons; for what son is he whom the father chasteneth not? (Hebrews 12:6-7)

Children

Jesus said unto them, Suffer the little children to come unto me, and forbid them not: for of such is the kingdom of God. (Mark 10:14)

Thou knowest the commandments, ..Do not steal, Do not bear false witness, Honour thy father and thy mother (Luke 18:20)

Christ

Jesus saith unto him, I am the way, the truth, and the life: no man cometh unto the Father, but by me.
(John 14:6)

This is a faithful saying, and worthy of all acceptation, that Christ Jesus came into the world to save sinners; of whom I am chief. (1 Timothy 1:15)

For there is one God, and one mediator between God and men, the man Christ Jesus; (1 Timothy 2:5)

I Am The Way, The Truth, And The Life.

The Baptism Of Jesus By John The Baptist
By Ottavio Vannini 1585-1643

Christ Died For Us

God commendeth his love toward us, in that, while we were yet sinners, Christ died for us. (Romans 5:8)

Christ Oriented

Let the word of Christ dwell in you richly in all wisdom; teaching and admonishing one another in psalms and hymns and spiritual songs, singing with grace in your hearts to the Lord.

And whatsoever ye do in word or deed, do all in the name of the Lord Jesus, giving thanks to God and the Father by him. (Colossians 3:16-17)

Whatsoever Ye Do, Do All In The Name Of The Lord Jesus.

Christ's Followers

He said to them all, If any man will come after me, let him deny himself, and take up his cross daily, and follow me. (Luke 9:23)

For whosoever will save his life shall lose it: but whosoever will lose his life for my sake, the same shall save it.

For what is a man advantaged, if he gain the whole world, and lose himself, or be cast away? (Luke 9:24-25)

Comfort

Come unto me, all ye that labour and are heavy laden, and I will give you rest. (Matthew 11:28)

And I will pray the Father, and he shall give you another Comforter, that he may abide with you for ever;
(John 14:16)

I Will Give You Rest.

The Spirit of truth, ye know him (the Holy Ghost); for he dwelleth with you, and shall be in you.

I will not leave you comfortless: I will come to you. (John 14:17-18)

Commandments, Great

Jesus said unto him, Thou shalt love the Lord thy God with all thy heart, and with all thy soul, and with all thy mind.

This is the first and great commandment.

And the second is like unto it, Thou shalt love thy neighbour as thyself.

On these two commandments hang all the law and the prophets. (Matthew 22:37-40)

Commandments, Ten

Please see **Ten Commandments.**

Commands Of Jesus

Jesus came and spake unto them, saying, All power is given unto me in heaven and in earth.

Go ye therefore, and teach all nations, baptizing them in the name of the Father, and of the Son, and of the Holy Ghost:

Teaching them to observe all things whatsoever I have commanded you: and, lo, I am with you alway, even unto the end of the world. Amen. (Matthew 28:18-20)

I Am With You Alway(s).

Commitment To Christ

If thou shalt confess with thy mouth the Lord Jesus, and shalt believe in thine heart that God hath raised him from the dead, thou shalt be saved.

For with the heart man believeth unto righteousness; and with the mouth confession is made unto salvation.

For the scripture saith, Whosoever believeth on him shall not be ashamed.

For there is no difference between the Jew and the Greek: for the same Lord over all is rich unto all that call upon him.

For whosoever shall call upon the name of the Lord shall be saved. (Romans 10:9-13)

Draw nigh to God, and he will draw nigh to you. Cleanse your hands, ye sinners; and purify your hearts, ye double minded.   (James 4:8)

Grow in grace, and in the knowledge of our Lord and Saviour Jesus Christ. To him be glory both now and for ever. Amen. (2 Peter 3:18)

Condemnation, Handling It

Blessed are ye, when men shall hate you, and when they shall separate you from their company, and shall reproach you, and cast out your name as evil, for the Son of man's sake.

Rejoice ye in that day, and leap for joy: for, behold, your reward is great in heaven: for in the like manner did their fathers unto the prophets.
(Luke 6:22-23)

For this is thankworthy, if a man for conscience toward God endure grief, suffering wrongfully.

Who his own self bare our sins in his own body on the tree (cross), that we, being dead to sins, should live unto righteousness: by whose stripes (Jesus') ye were healed. (1 Peter 2:19, 24)

Confession

If we confess our sins, he is faithful and just to forgive us our sins, and to cleanse us from all unrighteousness. (1 John 1:9)

Confess your faults one to another, and pray one for another, that ye may be healed. The effectual fervent prayer of a righteous man availeth much. (James 5:16)

Also I say unto you, Whosoever shall confess (acknowledge) me before men, him shall the Son of man also confess before the angels of God.
(Luke 12:8)

Contentment

Let your conversation be without covetousness; and be content with such things as ye have: for he hath said, I will never leave thee, nor forsake thee.
(Hebrews 13:5)

Therefore take no thought, saying, What shall we eat? or, What shall we drink? or, Wherewithal (by what means) shall we be clothed?
Your heavenly Father knoweth that ye have need of all these things.

But seek ye first the kingdom of God, and his righteousness; and all these things shall be added unto you. (Matthew 6:31-33)

And the peace of God, which passeth all understanding, shall keep your hearts and minds through Christ Jesus. (Philippians 4:7)

For I reckon that the sufferings of this present time are not worthy to be compared with the glory which shall be revealed in us. (Romans 8:18)

Contrition (Repentance)

Bring forth therefore fruits meet (appropriate) for repentance. (Matthew 3:8)

Go ye and learn what that meaneth, I will have mercy, and not sacrifice: for I am not come to call the righteous, but sinners to repentance. (Matthew 9:13)

Jesus saith unto them, They that are whole have no need of the physician, but they that are sick: I came not to call the righteous, but sinners to repentance. (Mark 2:17)

And he came into all the country about Jordan, preaching the baptism of repentance for the remission of sins; (Luke 3:3)

And that repentance and remission of sins should be preached in his name among all nations, beginning at Jerusalem. (Luke 24:47)

The Lord is not slack concerning his promise, as some men count slackness; but is longsuffering to usward (toward us), not willing that any should perish, but that all should come to repentance. (2 Peter 3:9)

Courage

I can do all things through Christ which strengtheneth me.
(Philippians 4:13)

Covetousness

He said unto them, Take heed, and beware of covetousness: for a man's life consisteth not in the abundance of the things which he possesseth.
(Luke 12:15)

Crown Of Righteousness

Henceforth there is laid up for me a crown of righteousness, which the Lord, the righteous judge, shall give me at that day: and not to me only, but unto all them also that love his appearing. (2 Timothy 4:8)

Death

Jesus said, I am the resurrection, and the life: he that believeth in me, though he were dead, yet shall he live:

And whosoever liveth and believeth in me shall never die. Believest thou this? (John 11:25-26)

In my Father's house are many mansions: if it were not so, I would have told you. I go to prepare a place for you.

And if I go and prepare a place for you, I will come again, and receive you unto myself; that where I am, there ye may be also. (John 14:2-3)

Deliver Me From Evil

The Lord is faithful, who shall stablish (establish) you, and keep you from evil. (2 Thessalonians 3:3)

The Lord shall deliver me from every evil work, and will preserve me unto his heavenly kingdom: to whom be glory for ever and ever. Amen.
(2 Timothy 4:18)

Denial Of Self

No man can serve two masters: for either he will hate the one, and love the other; or else he will hold to the one, and despise the other. Ye cannot serve God and mammon (materialism). (Matthew 6:24)

Despair, Conquering It

Come unto me, all ye that labour and are heavy laden, and I will give you rest. (Matthew 11:28)

Let your conversation be without covetousness; and be content with such things as ye have: for he hath said, I will never leave thee, nor forsake thee.

So that we may boldly say, The Lord is my helper, and I will not fear what man shall do unto me. (Hebrews 13:5-6)

Doers Of The Word

Be ye doers of the word, and not hearers only, deceiving your own selves. (James 1:22)

Doing God's Work

Lay not up for yourselves treasures upon earth, where moth and rust doth corrupt (decay), and where thieves break through and steal:

But lay up for yourselves treasures in heaven, where neither moth nor rust doth corrupt, and where thieves do not break through nor steal:
(Matthew 6:19-20)

Lay Up For Yourselves Treasures In Heaven.

Eat

Man shall not live by bread alone, but by every word that proceedeth out of the mouth of God.   (Matthew 4:4)

Effective Prayer

I say unto you, Ask, and it shall be given you; seek, and ye shall find; knock, and it shall be opened unto you. (Luke 11:9)

Likewise the Spirit also helpeth our infirmities: for we know not what we should pray for as we ought: but the Spirit itself maketh intercession for us with groanings which cannot be uttered. (Romans 8:26)

In every thing by prayer and supplication with thanksgiving let your requests be made known unto God.

And the peace of God, which passeth all understanding, shall keep (calm) your hearts and minds through Christ Jesus. (Philippians 4:6-7)

Let us therefore come boldly unto the throne of grace (God), that we may obtain mercy, and find grace to help in time of need. (Hebrews 4:16)

Confess your faults one to another, and pray one for another, that ye may be healed. The effectual fervent prayer of a righteous man availeth much. (James 5:16)

Come Boldly Unto The Throne Of Grace.

End (The Last Days)

This know also, that in the last days perilous times shall come.

For men shall be lovers of their own selves, covetous, boasters, proud, blasphemers, disobedient to parents, unthankful, unholy,

Without natural affection, trucebreakers, false accusers, incontinent, fierce, despisers of those that are good,

Traitors, heady, highminded, lovers of pleasures more than lovers of God;

Having a form of godliness, but denying the power thereof: from such turn away. (2 Timothy 3:1-5)

And on my servants and on my handmaidens I will pour out in those days of my Spirit; and they shall prophesy: (Acts 2:18)

And I will show wonders in heaven above, and signs in the earth beneath; blood, and fire, and vapour of smoke:

The sun shall be turned into darkness, and the moon into blood, before that great and notable day of the Lord come:

And it shall come to pass, that whosoever shall call on the name of the Lord shall be saved. (Acts 2:18-21)

Call On The Name Of The Lord.

Enemies

I say unto you which hear, Love your enemies, do good to them which hate you,

Bless them that curse you, and pray for them which despitefully use you. (Luke 6:27-28)

Entertain Strangers

Be not forgetful to entertain strangers: for thereby some have entertained angels unawares. (Hebrews 13:2)

Envy

Where envying and strife is, there is confusion and every evil work. (James 3:16)

Escape Condemnation

The word spoken by angels was stedfast (reliable), and every transgression and disobedience received a just recompense of reward;

How shall we escape, if we neglect so great salvation; which at the first began to be spoken by the Lord, and was confirmed unto us by them that heard him; (Hebrews 2:2-3)

Eternal Life

Verily, verily, I say unto you, He that heareth my word, and believeth on him that sent me, hath everlasting life, and shall not come into condemnation; but is passed from death unto life. (John 5:24)

Jesus said, I am the resurrection, and the life: he that believeth in me, though he were dead, yet shall he live:

And whosoever liveth and believeth in me shall never die. Believest thou this? (John 11:25-26)

I Am The Resurrection, And The Life.

So when this corruptible (person) shall have put on incorruption, and this mortal (person) shall have put on immortality, then shall be brought to pass the saying that is written, Death is swallowed up in (the) victory (of the resurrection). (1 Corinthians 15:54)

Evil

If ye then, being evil, know how to give good gifts unto your children: how much more shall your heavenly Father give the Holy Spirit to them that ask him? (Luke 11:13)

Faith

Jesus said unto them..verily I say unto you, If ye have faith as a grain of mustard seed, ye shall say unto this mountain, Remove hence to yonder place; and it shall remove; and nothing shall be impossible unto you. (Matthew 17:20)

Now faith is the substance of things hoped for, the evidence of things not seen.

Through faith we understand that the worlds were framed by the word of God, so that things which are seen were not made of things which do appear.

But without faith it is impossible to please him: for he that cometh to God must believe that he is, and that he is a rewarder of them that diligently seek him. (Hebrews 11:1, 3, 6)

Faith Is The Evidence Of Things Not Seen.

Fear

Let not your heart be troubled: ye believe in God, believe also in me. (John 14:1)

For God hath not given us the spirit of fear; but of power, and of love, and of a sound mind. (2 Timothy 1:7)

For the eyes of the Lord are over the righteous, and his ears are open unto their prayers: but the face of the Lord is against them that do evil.

And who is he that will harm you, if ye be followers of that which is good?

But and if ye suffer for righteousness' sake, happy are ye: and be not afraid of their terror, neither be troubled; (1 Peter 3:12-14)

Let Not Your Heart Be Troubled.

Fellowship of Believers

Ye are no more strangers and foreigners, but fellow citizens with the saints, and of the household of God;

And are built upon the foundation of the apostles and prophets, Jesus Christ himself being the chief corner stone; (Ephesians 2:19-20)

If we say that we have fellowship with him, and walk in darkness, we lie, and do not the truth:
But if we walk in the light, as he is in the light, we have fellowship one with another, and the blood of Jesus Christ his Son cleanseth us from all sin. (1 John 1:6-7)

Walk In The Light.

Finally, be ye all of one mind, having compassion one of another, love as brethren, be pitiful, be courteous: (1 Peter 3:8)

First And The Last

I am Alpha and Omega, the first and the last: and, What thou seest, write in a book, and send it unto the seven churches. (Revelation 1:11)

Fishers Of Men

Jesus, walking by the sea of Galilee, saw two brethren, Simon called Peter, and Andrew his brother, casting a net into the sea: for they were fishers.

And he saith unto them, Follow me, and I will make you fishers of men. (Matthew 4:18-19)

Follow Me

Jesus spake saying, I am the light of the world: he that followeth me shall not walk in darkness, but shall have the light of life. (John 8:12)

Forbearance

My beloved brethren, let every man be swift to hear, slow to speak, slow to wrath (anger):
For the wrath of man worketh not the righteousness of God.
(James 1:19-20)

But I say unto you, That ye resist not evil: but whosoever shall smite (strike) thee on thy right cheek, turn to him the other also. (Matthew 5:39)

Forgiveness

The righteousness of God is by faith of Jesus Christ unto all and upon all them that believe: for there is no difference:

For all have sinned, and come short of the glory of God;

Being justified freely by his grace through the redemption (salvation) that is in Christ Jesus:

Whom God hath set forth to be a propitiation (conciliation) through faith in his blood, to declare his righteousness for the remission of sins that are past, through the forbearance of God; (Romans 3:22-25)

And be ye kind one to another, tenderhearted, forgiving one another, even as God for Christ's sake hath forgiven you. (Ephesians 4:32)

Freedom From The Bondage Of Sin

Brethren, ye have been called unto liberty; only use not liberty for an occasion to the flesh (self-indulgence to do wrong) but by love serve one another.   (Galatians 5:13)

Freedom In Christ

Ye shall know the truth, and the truth shall make you free (from sin).

If the Son therefore shall make you free, ye shall be free indeed. (John 8:32-36)

Because the creature (person) itself also shall be delivered from the bondage of corruption into the glorious liberty of the children of God. (Romans 8:21)

For though I be free from all men, yet have I made myself servant unto all, that I might gain the more.
(1 Corinthians 9:19)

There is neither Jew nor Greek, there is neither bond (slave) nor free, there is neither male nor female: for ye are all one in Christ Jesus.
(Galatians 3:28)

Fruitfulness

I am the vine, ye are the branches: He that abideth in me, and I in him, the same bringeth forth much fruit: for without me ye can do nothing.

If ye abide in me, and my words abide in you, ye shall ask what ye will, and it shall be done unto you.
(John 15:5,7)

Herein is my Father glorified, that ye bear much fruit; so shall ye be my disciples.   (John 15:8)

Fruit Of The Spirit

The fruit of the Spirit (Divine Influence, God) is love, joy, peace, longsuffering, gentleness, goodness, faith, (Galatians 5:22)

If we live in the Spirit, let us also walk in the Spirit. (Galatians 5:25)

Gifts Of God

God hath not given us the spirit of fear; but of power, and of love, and of a sound mind. (2 Timothy 1:7)

Glorify God

With one mind and one mouth glorify God, even the Father of our Lord Jesus Christ. (Romans 15:6)

Glory Of God

I pray that your love may abound yet more and more in knowledge and in all judgment;

Being filled with the fruits of righteousness, which are by Jesus Christ, unto (to) the glory and praise of God. (Philippians 1:9-11)

Blessed be the God and Father of our Lord Jesus Christ, which according to his abundant mercy hath begotten (created) us again unto a lively hope by the resurrection of Jesus Christ from the dead, (1 Peter 1:3)

The God of all grace, who hath called us unto his eternal glory by Christ Jesus, after that ye have suffered a while, make you perfect, stablish (establish), strengthen, settle you. (1 Peter 5:10)

God Is One

There is one body, and one Spirit, even as ye are called in one hope of your calling;

One Lord, one faith, one baptism,

One God and Father of all, who is above all, and through all, and in you all. (Ephesians 4:4-6)

God Seeking

Without faith it is impossible to please him: for he that cometh to God must believe that he is, and that he is a rewarder of them that diligently seek him.   (Hebrews 11:6)

Also see **Seeking God.**

God's Gifts To Us

If ye then, being evil, know how to give good gifts unto your children, how much more shall your Father which is in heaven give good things to them that ask him?   (Matthew 7:11)

He that spared not his own Son, but delivered him up for us all, how shall he not with him also freely give us all things? (Romans 8:32)

God's Help In Trouble

If ye shall ask any thing in my name, I will do it. (John 14:14)

And he said unto me, My grace is sufficient for thee: for my strength is made perfect in weakness. Most gladly therefore will I rather glory in my infirmities, that the power of Christ may rest upon me. (2 Corinthians 12:9)

My Grace Is Sufficient For Thee.

God's Love For Us

God so loved the world, that he gave his only begotten Son, that whosoever believeth in him should not perish, but have everlasting life. (John 3:16)

And we have known and believed the love that God hath to us. God is love; and he that dwelleth in love dwelleth in God, and God in him.
(1 John 4:16)

God's Personality

If we confess our sins, he is faithful and just to forgive us our sins, and to cleanse us from all unrighteousness.
(1 John 1:9)

The foolishness of God is wiser than men; and the weakness of God is stronger than men. (1 Corinthians 1:25)

Every good gift and every perfect gift is from above, and cometh down from the Father of lights, with whom is no variableness, neither shadow of turning.   (James 1:17)

God's Power

Jesus beheld them, and said unto them, With men this is impossible; but with God all things are possible. (Matthew 19:26)

If God be for us, who can be against us? (Romans 8:31

I can do all things through Christ which strengtheneth me. (Philippians 4:13)

If God Be For Us, Who Can Be Against Us?

Golden Rule

All things whatsoever ye would that men should do to you, do ye even so to them: for this is the law and the prophets.   (Matthew 7:12)

Good, All Things For

We know that all things work together for good to them that love God, to them who are the called according to his purpose. (Romans 8:28)

Inasmuch As Ye Have Done It Unto One Of The Least Of These My Brethren, Ye Have Done It Unto Me.

The Good Samaritan Bringing The Injured Man To The Inn
By Gustave Doré
The Doré Bible Illustrations, Dover Publications, Inc.

Good Samaritan

Jesus said, A certain man went down from Jerusalem to Jericho, and fell among thieves, which stripped him of his raiment (clothing), and wounded him, and departed, leaving him half dead.

But a certain Samaritan, as he journeyed, came where he was: and when he saw him, he had compassion on him,

And went to him, and bound up his wounds, pouring in oil and wine, and set him on his own beast, and brought him to an inn, and took care of him.

And on the morrow when he departed, he took out two pence, and gave them to the host, and said unto him, Take care of him; and whatsoever thou spendest more, when I come again, I will repay thee. (Luke 10:30, 33-35)

Grace

Even when we were dead in sins, (God) hath quickened (revived) us together with Christ,

For by grace are ye saved through faith; and that not of yourselves: it is the gift of God: (Ephesians 2:5,8)

But unto every one of us is given grace according to the measure of the gift of Christ. (Ephesians 4:7)

Guidance

I am the good shepherd: the good shepherd giveth his life for the sheep. (John 10:11)

The Lord shall deliver me from every evil work, and will preserve me

unto his heavenly kingdom: to whom be glory for ever and ever. Amen.
(2 Timothy 4:18)

Guilt

God commendeth his love toward us, in that, while we were yet sinners, Christ died for us. (Romans 5:8)

If we confess our sins, he is faithful and just to forgive us our sins, and to cleanse us from all unrighteousness.
(1 John 1:9)

Harmony

A new commandment I give unto you, That ye love one another; as I have loved you, that ye also love one another.

By this shall all men know that ye are my disciples, if ye have love one to another. (John 13:34-35)

Healing And Health

Behold, there was a woman which had a spirit of infirmity (was sick) eighteen years, and was bowed together, and could in no wise lift up herself.

And when Jesus saw her, he called her to him, and said unto her, Woman, thou art loosed (cured) from thine infirmity.   (Luke 13:11-12)

Likewise the Spirit also helpeth our infirmities: for we know not what we should pray for as we ought: but the Spirit itself maketh intercession for us with groanings (painful sounds) which cannot be uttered. (Romans 8:26)

And the prayer of faith shall save the sick, and the Lord shall raise him up; and if he have committed sins, they shall be forgiven him. (James 5:15)

Help From God

Please see Ability.

Helping Others

All things whatsoever ye would that men should do to you, do ye even so to them: for this is the law and the prophets.
(The Golden Rule, Matthew 7:12)

Verily I say unto you, Inasmuch as ye have done it unto one of the least of these my brethren, ye have done it unto me. (Matthew 25:40)

It Is More Blessed To Give Than To Receive.

Holy Spirit

I will pray the Father, and he shall give you another Comforter, that he may abide with you for ever;

Even the Spirit of truth; .. ye know him; for he dwelleth with you, and shall be in you. (John 14:16-17)

It is expedient for you that I go away: for if I go not away, the Comforter will not come unto you; but if I depart, I will send him unto you.

And when he is come, he will reprove (correct) the world of sin, and of righteousness, and of judgment:
(John 16:7-8)

But if the Spirit of him that raised up Jesus from the dead dwell in you, he that raised up Christ from the dead shall also quicken (revive) your mortal bodies by his Spirit that dwelleth in you.
(Romans 8:11)

Honesty

All things whatsoever ye would that men should do to you, do ye even so to them: for this is the law and the prophets. (Matthew 7:12)

I exhort (urge) therefore, that, first of all, supplications, prayers, intercessions, and giving of thanks, be made for all men;

For kings, and for all that are in authority; that we may lead a quiet and peaceable life in all godliness and honesty.

For this is good and acceptable in the sight of God our Saviour;
(1 Timothy 2:1-3)

I Exhort Prayers For All Men.

Hope

We are saved by hope: but hope that is seen is not hope: for what a man seeth, why doth he yet hope for?

But if we hope for that we see not, then do we with patience wait for it. (Romans 8:24-25)

Now the God of hope fill you with all joy and peace in believing, that ye may abound in hope, through the power of the Holy Ghost.
(Romans 15:13)

Blessed be the God and Father of our Lord Jesus Christ, which according to his abundant mercy hath begotten us (made us born) again unto a lively hope by the resurrection of Jesus Christ from the dead. (1 Peter 1:3)

Ye were not redeemed with corruptible things, but with the

precious blood of Christ, as of a lamb without blemish and without spot:

Who by him (Christ) do (you) believe in God, that raised him up from the dead, and gave him glory; that your faith and hope might be in God.
(1 Peter 1:18,19,21)

Hospitality

I was an hungered, and ye gave me meat: I was thirsty, and ye gave me drink: I was a stranger, and ye took me in:

Naked, and ye clothed me: I was sick, and ye visited me: I was in prison, and ye came unto me.
(Matthew 25:35-36)

Verily I say unto you, Inasmuch as ye have done it unto one of the least of these my brethren, ye have done it unto me. (Matthew 25:40)

Be not forgetful to entertain strangers: for thereby some have entertained angels unawares.
(Hebrews 13:2)

Humility

Humble yourselves under the mighty hand of God, that he may exalt you in due time: (1 Peter 5:6)

Also see **Meekness.**

Hunger

Take no thought, saying, What shall we eat? or, What shall we drink? or, Wherewithal (by what means) shall we be clothed?

I Am The Bread Of Life.
Jesus Blessing And Giving The Bread And Wine,
His Body And Blood, To His Disciples
Detail From Painting Of The Last Supper
By Paolo Veronese 1528-88

Your heavenly Father knoweth that ye have need of all these things.

But seek ye first the kingdom of God, and his righteousness; and all these things shall be added unto you. (Matthew 6:31-33)

And Jesus said unto them, I am the bread of life: he that cometh to me shall never hunger; and he that believeth on me shall never thirst. (John 6:35)

Husbands and Wives

Wives, submit yourselves unto your own husbands, as unto the Lord.

For the husband is the head of the wife, even as Christ is the head of the church: and he is the saviour of the body.

Therefore as the church is subject unto Christ, so let the wives be to their own husbands in every thing.

Husbands, love your wives, even as Christ also loved the church, and gave himself for it; (Ephesians 5:22-25)

So ought men to love their wives as their own bodies. He that loveth his wife loveth himself.

For no man ever yet hated his own flesh; but nourisheth and cherisheth it, even as the Lord the church:

For we are members of his body, of his flesh, and of his bones.

For this cause shall a man leave his father and mother, and shall be joined unto his wife, and they two shall be one flesh.

This is a great mystery:

Nevertheless let every one of you in particular so love his wife even as

himself; and the wife see that she reverence (honor) her husband.
(Ephesians 5:28-33)

Inspiration from God

From a child thou hast known the holy scriptures, which are able to make thee wise unto salvation through faith which is in Christ Jesus.

All scripture is given by inspiration of God, and is profitable for doctrine, for reproof, for correction, for instruction in righteousness:
(2 Timothy 3:15-16)

Jealousy

Please see **Envy**.

Jesus

Jesus saith unto him, I am the way, the truth, and the life: no man cometh unto the Father, but by me.
(John 14:6)

God commendeth (acclaimed) his love toward us, in that, while we were yet sinners, Christ died for us.
Much more then, being now justified by his (Christ's) blood, we shall be saved from wrath (anger) through him.

We were reconciled to God by the death of his Son, much more, being reconciled, we shall be saved by his life.
We also joy in God through our Lord Jesus Christ, by whom we have now received the atonement.
(Romans 5:8-11)

For there is one God, and one mediator between God and men, the man Christ Jesus; (1 Timothy 2:5)

Jesus the author and finisher of our faith; who for the joy that was set before him endured the cross, despising the shame, and is set down at the right hand of the throne of God.
(Hebrews 12:2)

Joy

I have spoken unto you, that my joy might remain in you, and that your joy might be full. (John 15:11)

Whom having not seen (Jesus), ye love; in whom, though now ye see him not, yet believing, ye rejoice with joy unspeakable and full of glory: (1 Peter 1:8)

Judge Not

Judge not, that ye be not judged.
For with what judgment ye judge, ye shall be judged: and with what measure ye mete (give), it shall be measured to you again. (Matthew 7:1-2)

Rejoice With Joy Unspeakable.

Judgment Seat

Every one of us shall give account of himself to God.
(Romans 14:12)

For we must all appear before the judgment seat of Christ; that every one may receive the things done in his body, according to that he hath done, whether it be good or bad. (2 Corinthians 5:10)

Be not deceived; God is not mocked: for whatsoever a man soweth (plants), that shall he also reap (get).

For he that soweth to his flesh shall of the flesh reap corruption; but he that soweth to the Spirit shall of the Spirit reap life everlasting.
(Galatians 6:7-8)

He That Soweth To The Spirit Shall Reap Life Everlasting.

Kingdom Of God

Seek ye first the kingdom of God, and his righteousness; and all (these) things shall be added unto you. (Matthew 6:33)

For the kingdom of God is not meat and drink; but righteousness, and peace, and joy in the Holy Ghost. (Romans 14:17)

Kingship Of God

With God nothing shall be impossible. (Luke 1:37)

And when I saw him, I fell at his feet as dead. And he laid his right hand upon me, saying unto me, Fear not; I am the first and the last:

I am he that liveth, and was dead; and, behold, I am alive for evermore, Amen; and have the keys of hell and of death. (Revelation 1:17-18)

Also see **Kingship of God** in **Psalms**

Laborers

We are labourers together with God: ye are God's husbandry (harvest), ye are God's building.
(1 Corinthians 3:9)

Laziness

Be kindly affectioned one to another with brotherly love; in honour preferring one another;

Not slothful (lazy) in business; fervent in spirit; serving the Lord; (Romans 12:10-11)

Life Everlasting

He that findeth his life shall lose it: and he that loseth his life for my sake shall find it. (Matthew 10:39)

For God so loved the world, that he gave his only begotten Son, that whosoever believeth in him should not perish, but have everlasting life.
(John 3:16)

He that believeth on the Son hath everlasting life: and he that believeth not the Son shall not see life; but the wrath (anger) of God abideth (stays) on him.
(John 3:36)

But these are written, that ye might believe that Jesus is the Christ, the Son of God; and that believing ye might have life through his name.
(John 20:31)

Live

Jesus answered, saying, It is written, That man shall not live by bread alone, but by every word of God.
(Luke 4:4)

Loneliness

I will not leave you comfortless: I will come to you. (John 14:18)

And all things are of God, who hath reconciled (made acceptable) us to himself by Jesus Christ, and hath given to us the ministry of reconciliation;
(2 Corinthians 5:18)

And (I) will be a Father unto you, and ye shall be my sons and daughters, saith the Lord Almighty.
(2 Corinthians 6:18)

Long Life

Honour thy father and mother; which is the first commandment with promise;

That it may be well with thee, and thou mayest live long on the earth. (Ephesians 6:2-3)

Lord's Prayer

Please see pages 17 and 18.

Love

I say unto you, Love your enemies, bless them that curse you, do good to them that hate you, and pray for them which despitefully use you, and persecute you; (Matthew 5:44)

If ye keep my commandments, ye shall abide (remain) in my love; even as

I have kept my Father's commandments, and abide in his love.

These things have I spoken unto you, that my joy might remain in you, and that your joy might be full.

This is my commandment, That ye love one another, as I have loved you.

Greater love hath no man than this, that a man lay down his life for his friends. (John 15:10-13)

And this I pray, that your love may abound yet more and more in knowledge and in all judgment; (Philippians 1:9)

Love Of God For Us

God so loved the world, that he gave his only begotten Son,

that whosoever believeth in him should not perish, but have everlasting life. (John 3:16)

What is man, that thou art mindful of him? or the son of man, that thou visitest him?
Thou madest him a little lower than the angels; thou crownedst him with glory and honour, and didst set him over the works of thy hands:
(Hebrews 2:6-7)

Loving God

Jesus said unto him, Thou shalt love the Lord thy God with all thy heart, and with all thy soul, and with all thy mind.   (Matthew 22:37)

He that hath my commandments, and keepeth them, he it is that loveth me: and he that loveth me shall be loved of my Father, and I will love him, and will manifest myself to him.(John 14:21)

Grace be with all them that love our Lord Jesus Christ in sincerity. Amen. (Ephesians 6:24)

Lust

Ye lust (crave), and have not: ye kill, and desire to have, and cannot obtain: ye fight and war, yet ye have not, because ye ask not.

Ye ask, and receive not, because ye ask amiss (in error), that ye may consume it upon your lusts. (James 4:2-3)

Flee also youthful lusts: but follow righteousness, faith, charity, peace, with them that call on the Lord out of a pure heart. (2 Timothy 2:22)

Lying

Lie not one to another, seeing that ye have put off the old man with his deeds;

And have put on the new man, which is renewed in knowledge (of righteousness) after the image of him (God) that created him: (Colossians 3:9-10)

Man, What Is Man?

See **Love of God for Us**.

Mansions Of God

In my Father's house are many mansions: if it were not so, I would have told you. I go to prepare a place for you. (John 14:2)

And if I go and prepare a place for you, I will come again, and receive you unto myself; that where I am, there ye may be also. (John 14:3)

Marriage

Let the husband render unto the wife due benevolence: and likewise also the wife unto the husband.
(1 Corinthians 7:3)

Wives, submit yourselves unto your own husbands, as unto the Lord.

For the husband is the head of the wife, even as Christ is the head of the church: and he is the saviour of the body.

Therefore as the church is subject unto Christ, so let the wives be to their own husbands in every thing.

Husbands, love your wives, even as Christ also loved the church, and gave himself for it; (Ephesians 5:22-25)

Mary

The birth of Jesus Christ was on this wise: When as his mother Mary was espoused to Joseph, before they came together, she was found with child of the Holy Ghost.

Then Joseph her husband, being a just man, and not willing to make her a public example, was minded to put her away privily (secretly).

But while he thought on these things, behold, the angel of the Lord appeared unto him in a dream, saying, Joseph, thou son of David, fear not to take unto thee Mary thy wife: for that which is conceived in her is of the Holy Ghost.

And she shall bring forth a son, and thou shalt call his name Jesus: for he shall save his people from their sins.

Now all this was done, that it might be fulfilled which was spoken of the Lord by the prophet, saying,

Behold, a virgin shall be with child, and shall bring forth a son, and they shall call his name Emmanuel, which being interpreted is, God with us.

Then Joseph being raised from sleep did as the angel of the Lord had bidden him, and took unto him his wife:

And knew her not till she had brought forth her firstborn son: and he called his name Jesus.
(Matthew 1:18-25)

Emmanuel, God With Us.

Meekness

Blessed are the meek: for they shall inherit the earth. (Matthew 5:5)

And unto him that smiteth (strikes) thee on the one cheek offer also the other; and him that taketh away thy cloak forbid not to take thy coat also. (Luke 6:29)

Mercy

Blessed are the merciful: for they shall obtain mercy. (Matthew 5:7)

Be ye therefore merciful, as your Father also is merciful.

Judge not, and ye shall not be judged: condemn not, and ye shall not be condemned: forgive, and ye shall be forgiven:

Give, and it shall be given unto you...with the same measure that ye mete (distribute) withal (with that) it shall be measured to you again.
(Luke 6:36-38)

Mind Of God

Who hath known the mind of the Lord, that he may instruct him? But we have the mind of Christ.
(1 Corinthians 2:16)

Money

Lay up for yourselves treasures in heaven, where neither moth nor rust doth corrupt, and where thieves do not break through nor steal:
(Matthew 6:20)

Then saith (says) he unto them, Render therefore unto Caesar the things which are Caesar's; and unto God the things that are God's. (Matthew 22:21)

My God shall supply all your need according to his riches in glory by Christ Jesus. (Philippians 4:19)

The love of money is the root of all evil: which while some coveted after, they have erred (strayed) from the faith, and pierced themselves through with many sorrows. (1 Timothy 6:10)

Mustard Seed

Another parable (symbolism) put he forth unto them, saying, The kingdom of heaven is like to a grain of mustard seed, which a man took, and sowed (planted) in his field: (Matthew 13:31)

Which indeed is the least of all seeds: but when it is grown, it is the greatest among herbs, and becometh a tree, (Matthew 13:32)

And Jesus said unto them...verily I say unto you, If ye have faith as a grain of mustard seed, ye shall say unto this mountain, Remove hence to yonder place; and it shall remove; and nothing shall be impossible unto you. (Matthew 17:20)

Near To God

Draw nigh (near) to God, and he will draw nigh to you. Cleanse your hands, ye sinners; and purify your hearts, ye double minded (undecided). (James 4:8)

Humble yourselves in the sight of the Lord, and he shall lift you up. (James 4:10)

Obedience To God

Whosoever shall do the will of my Father which is in heaven, the same is my brother, and sister, and mother. (Matthew 12:50)

If ye keep my commandments, ye shall abide (remain) in my love; even as I have kept my Father's commandments, and abide in his love. (John 15:10)

And the world passeth away, and the lust thereof: but he that doeth the will of God abideth for ever. (1 John 2:17)

See also the **Ten Commandments**.

Jesus Carrying His Cross
He showed his obedience to the Will of God.
God gave his only begotten son to save us.

By El Greco 1548-1614

Old Age

He which raised up the Lord Jesus shall raise up us also by Jesus, (2 Corinthians 4:14)

We faint not; though our outward (physical) man perish, yet the inward (spiritual) man is renewed day by day.

For our light affliction, which is but for a moment, worketh (makes) for us a far more exceeding and eternal weight of glory;

While we look not at the things which are seen, but at the things which are not seen: for the things which are seen are temporal; but the things which are not seen are eternal.
(2 Corinthians 4:16-18)

Also see **Old Age** in **Psalms**.

Overcoming The World

Whatsoever is born of God overcometh the world: and this is the victory that overcometh the world, even our faith.

Who is he that overcometh the world, but he that believeth that Jesus is the Son of God? (1 John 5:4-5)

Patience

In your patience possess ye your souls. (Luke 21:19)

Be patient therefore, brethren, unto the coming of the Lord. Behold, the husbandman (farmer) waiteth for the precious fruit of the earth, and hath long patience for it, until he receive the early and latter rain. (James 5:7)

For ye have need of patience, that, after ye have done the will of God, ye might receive the promise.
(Hebrews 10:36)

> Also read **Courage**
> in **Psalms**

Peace

Peace I leave with you, my peace I give unto you: not as the world giveth, give I unto you. Let not your heart be troubled, neither let it be afraid.
(John 14:27)

And the peace of God, which passeth all understanding, shall keep your hearts and minds through Christ Jesus.
(Philippians 4:7)

Persecution

Blessed are ye, when men shall revile (speak abusively about) you, and persecute you, and shall say all manner of evil against you falsely, for my sake.

Rejoice, and be exceeding glad: for great is your reward in heaven: for so persecuted they the prophets which were before you. (Matthew 5:11-12)

Pleasing God

Please see **God Seeking.**

When Men Persecute You For My Sake, Rejoice; Great Is Your Reward In Heaven.

Poverty

Ask, and it shall be given you; seek, and ye shall find; knock, and it shall be opened unto you:

For every one that asketh receiveth; and he that seeketh findeth; and to him that knocketh it shall be opened.

If ye then, being evil, know how to give good gifts unto your children, how much more shall your Father which is in heaven give good things to them that ask him?   (Matthew 7:7,8,11)

And all things, whatsoever ye shall ask in prayer, believing, ye shall receive.   (Matthew 21:22)

Power Of God

Please see **God's Power**

Praising God

It came to pass, that as he was come nigh unto Jericho (North of Dead Sea), a certain blind man sat by the way side begging:

And he cried, saying, Jesus, thou son of David, have mercy on me.

And Jesus stood, and commanded him to be brought unto him: and when he was come near, he asked him,

Saying, What wilt thou that I shall do unto thee? And he said, Lord, that I may receive my sight.

And Jesus said unto him, Receive thy sight: thy faith hath saved thee.

And immediately he received his sight, and followed him, glorifying God: and all the people, when they saw it, gave praise unto God.
(Luke 18:35,38,40,41,42,43)

And when he was come nigh (near), even now at the descent of the Mount of Olives (E. of Jerusalem), the whole multitude of the disciples began to rejoice and praise God with a loud voice for all the mighty works that they had seen; (Luke 19:37)

Praise the Lord, all ye people. (Romans 15:11)

Prayer, The Lord's

When thou prayest, enter into thy closet, and when thou hast shut thy door, pray to thy Father which is in secret; and thy Father which seeth in secret shall reward thee openly.

After this manner therefore pray ye: Our Father which art in heaven, Hallowed (Holy) be thy name... (Matthew 6:6-9)

Please see the **Lord's Prayer**.

Verily, verily, I say unto you, Whatsoever ye shall ask the Father in my name, he will give it you.

Hitherto (until now) have ye asked nothing in my name: ask, and ye shall receive, that your joy may be full. (John 16:23-24)

Pride

He sat down, and called the twelve, and saith unto them, If any man desire to be first, the same shall be last of all, and servant of all. (Mark 9:35)

Humble yourselves therefore under the mighty hand of God, that he may exalt you in due time: (1 Peter 5:6)

What Ye Ask In My Name, He Will Give You.

Prodigal Son

The younger of them said to his father, Father, give me the portion of goods that falleth to me (my inheritance). And he divided unto them his living. And not many days after the younger son gathered all together, and took his journey into a far country, and there wasted his substance (possessions) with riotous living.

I will arise and go to my father, and will say unto him, Father, I have sinned against heaven, and before thee,

And am no more worthy to be called thy son: make me as one of thy hired servants.

And he arose, and came to his father. But when he was yet a great way off, his father saw him, and had compassion, and ran, and fell on his neck, and kissed him. (Luke 15:12,13,18,19,20)

And the son said unto him, Father, I have sinned against heaven, and in thy sight, and am no more worthy to be called thy son.

But the father said to his servants, Bring forth the best robe, and put it on him; and put a ring on his hand, and shoes on his feet: And bring hither the fatted (well-fed) calf, and kill it; and let us eat, and be merry:

For this my son was dead, and is alive again; he was lost, and is found. And they began to be merry.

And he said unto him, Son, thou art ever with me, and all that I have is thine.

It was meet (appropriate) that we should make merry, and be glad: for this thy brother was dead, and is alive again; and was lost, and is found.
(Luke15:21-24,31-32)

Promises Of The Bible

Heaven and earth shall pass away, but my words shall not pass away. (Matthew 24:35)

For with God nothing shall be impossible. (Luke 1:37)

God so loved the world, that he gave his only begotten Son, that whosoever believeth in him should not perish, but have everlasting life.

God sent not his Son into the world to condemn the world; but that the world through him might be saved. (John 3:16-17)

Whereby are given unto us exceeding great and precious promises: that by these ye might be partakers of the divine nature (become children of God), having escaped the corruption

that is in the world through lust.
(2 Peter 1:4)

>Also see **Peace**.

Prosperity

Your heavenly Father knoweth that ye have need of all these things (which you ask).

But seek ye first the kingdom of God, and his righteousness; and all these things shall be added unto you.
(Matthew 6:32-33)

Protection

The peace of God, which passeth (is beyond) all understanding, shall keep your hearts and minds through Christ Jesus. (Philippians 4:7)

For the eyes of the Lord are over the righteous, and his ears are open unto their prayers: but the face of the Lord is against them that do evil.

And who is he that will harm you, if ye be followers of that which is good? (1 Peter 3:12-13)

The Eyes Of The Lord Are Over The Righteous.

Receiving What You Ask

I say unto you, Ask, and it shall be given you; seek, and ye shall find; knock, and it shall be opened unto you.

For every one that asketh receiveth; and he that seeketh findeth; and to him that knocketh it shall be opened. (Luke 11:9-10)

Repentance

I say unto you, that likewise joy shall be in heaven over one sinner that repenteth, more than over ninety and nine just persons, which need no repentance. (Luke 15:7)

Brethren, if any of you do err from the truth, and one convert him;
Let him know, that he which converteth the sinner from the error of his way shall save a soul from death, and shall hide a multitude of sins. (James 5:19-20)

Rest

Come unto me, all ye that labour and are heavy laden, and I will give you rest.
Take my yoke upon you (join me), and learn of me; for I am meek and

lowly in heart: and ye shall find rest unto your souls.
For my yoke (harness) is easy, and my burden is light.
(Matthew 11:28-30)

Resurrection
Jesus said..I am the resurrection, and the life: he that believeth in me, though he were dead, yet shall he live: And whosoever liveth and believeth in me shall never die. (John 11:25-26)

Revenge
Vengeance is mine; I will repay, saith the Lord. (Romans 12:19)

Revival
The Lord is not slack concerning his promise, but is longsuffering to usward (toward us), not willing that any

should perish, but that all should come to repentance. (2 Peter 3:9)

Reward for Righteousness

Peter said unto him, behold, we have forsaken all, and followed thee; what shall we have therefore?

And Jesus said unto them, Verily I say unto you, That ye which have followed me, in the regeneration (resurrection) when the Son of man shall sit in the throne of his glory, ye also shall sit upon twelve thrones, judging the twelve tribes of Israel. (Matthew 19:27-28)

Take no thought, saying, What shall we eat? or, What shall we drink? or, Wherewithal shall we be clothed?

But seek ye first the kingdom of God, and his righteousness; and all these things shall be added unto you. (Matthew 6:31, 33)

Rich Man

It is easier for a camel to go through a needle's eye, than for a rich man to enter into the kingdom of God. (Luke 18:25)

Man Shall Not Live By Bread Alone.

Sadness, Coping With It

The Lamb which is in the midst of the throne shall feed them, and shall lead them unto living fountains of waters: and God shall wipe away all tears from their eyes. (Revelation 7:17)

God Shall Wipe Away All Tears.

Salvation

Jesus said, Verily, verily, I say unto thee, Except a man be born again, he cannot see the kingdom of God.

For God sent not his Son into the world to condemn the world; but that the world through him might be saved.

Verily, verily, I say unto you, He that heareth my word, and believeth on him that sent me, hath everlasting life, and shall not come into condemnation; but is passed from death unto life. (John 5:3,17,24)

If thou shalt confess with thy mouth (acknowledge) the Lord Jesus, and shalt believe in thine heart that God hath raised him from the dead, thou shalt be saved. (Romans 10:9)

Confess Jesus And Be Saved.

For by grace are ye saved through faith; and that not of yourselves: it is the gift of God: (Ephesians 2:8)

And take the helmet of salvation, and the sword of the Spirit, which is the word of God (to fight evil): (Ephesians 6:17)

But if we walk in the light, as he is in the light, we have fellowship one with another, and the blood of Jesus Christ his Son cleanseth us from all sin. (1 John 1:7)

Samaritan, Good

Please see **The Good Samaritan.**

By Grace Are Ye Saved Through Faith.

Seeking God

I say unto you, Ask, and it shall be given you; seek, and ye shall find; knock, and it shall be opened unto you.

For every one that asketh receiveth; and he that seeketh findeth; and to him that knocketh it shall be opened.

If a son shall ask bread of any of you that is a father, will he give him a stone? or if he ask a fish, will he for a fish give him a serpent?

Or if he shall ask an egg, will he offer him a scorpion?

If ye then, being evil, know how to give good gifts unto your children: how much more shall your heavenly Father give the Holy Spirit to them that ask him? (Luke 11:9-13)

Please also see **God Seeking.**

Self Worth

Are not five sparrows sold for two farthings (a small price), and not one of them is forgotten before God?

But even the very hairs of your head are all numbered. Fear not therefore: ye are of more value than many sparrows.   (Luke 12:6-7)

Sermon On The Mount
Including The
The Beatitudes
Matthew 5-7

This is the longest recorded utterance of our Lord. Its length and the subjects covered impart to it an outstanding power and significance. It is a statement of the Character of God's kingdom of heaven. It follows the next picture.

The Sermon On The Mount
By Gustave Doré
The Doré Bible Illustrations, Dover Publications, Inc.

The Sermon On The Mount

Seeing the multitudes, he went up into a mountain: and when he was set, his disciples came unto him:

And he opened his mouth, and taught them, saying,

Blessed (happy) are the poor in spirit: for theirs is the kingdom of heaven. Blessed are they that mourn: for they shall be comforted.

Blessed are the meek: for they shall inherit the earth.

Blessed are they which do hunger and thirst after righteousness: for they shall be filled.

Blessed are the merciful: for they shall obtain mercy.

Blessed are the pure in heart: for they shall see God.

Blessed are the peacemakers: for they shall be called the children of God.

The Sermon On The Mount continued:

Blessed are they which are persecuted for righteousness' sake: for theirs is the kingdom of heaven.

Blessed are ye, when men shall revile you, and persecute you, and shall say all manner of evil against you falsely, for my sake.

Rejoice, and be exceeding glad: for great is your reward in heaven: for so persecuted they the prophets which were before you.

Ye are the salt of the earth: but if the salt have lost his savour, wherewith shall it be salted? it is thenceforth good for nothing, but to be cast out, and to be trodden under foot of men.

Ye are the light of the world. A city that is set on an hill cannot be hid.

Neither do men light a candle, and put it under a bushel, but on a

The Sermon On The Mount continued:

candlestick; and it giveth light unto all that are in the house.

Let your light so shine before men, that they may see your good works, and glorify your Father which is in heaven.

Think not that I am come to destroy the law, or the prophets: I am not come to destroy, but to fulfill.

I say unto you, Till heaven and earth pass, one jot (least part) or one tittle (punctuation mark) shall in no wise pass from the law, till all be fulfilled.

Whosoever therefore shall break one of these least commandments, and shall teach men so, he shall be called the least in the kingdom of heaven: but whosoever shall do and teach them, the same shall be called great in the kingdom of heaven.

The Sermon On The Mount continued:

For I say unto you, That except your righteousness shall exceed the righteousness of the scribes and Pharisees, ye shall in no case enter into the kingdom of heaven.

Ye have heard that it was said by them of old time, Thou shalt not kill; and whosoever shall kill shall be in danger of the judgment:

But I say unto you, That whosoever is angry with his brother without a cause shall be in danger of the judgment: and whosoever shall say to his brother, Raca (Idiot), shall be in danger of the council: but whosoever shall say, Thou fool, shall be in danger of hell fire (of hell). Therefore if thou bring thy gift to the altar, and there rememberest that thy brother hath ought against thee (is upset with you);

The Sermon On The Mount continued:

Leave there thy gift before the altar, and go thy way; first be reconciled to thy brother, and then come and offer thy gift.

Agree with thine adversary (accuser) quickly, whiles (while) thou art in the way with him; lest at any time the adversary deliver thee to the judge, and the judge deliver thee to the officer, and thou be cast into prison.

Verily I say unto thee, Thou shalt by no means come out thence, till thou hast paid the uttermost farthing (final payment).

Ye have heard that it was said by them of old time, Thou shalt not commit adultery: But I say unto you, That whosoever looketh on a woman to lust after her hath committed adultery with her already in his heart.

The Sermon On The Mount continued:

And if thy right eye offend thee (causes you to sin), pluck it out, and cast it from thee: for it is profitable for thee that one of thy members should perish, and not that thy whole body should be cast into hell.

And if thy right hand offend thee, cut it off, and cast it from thee: for it is profitable for thee that one of thy members should perish, and not that thy whole body should be cast into hell.

It hath been said, Whosoever shall put away his wife, let him give her a writing of divorcement:

But I say unto you, That whosoever shall put away (divorce) his wife, saving for the cause of fornication, causeth her to commit adultery: and whosoever shall marry her that is divorced committeth adultery.

The Sermon On The Mount continued:

Again, ye have heard that it hath been said by them of old time, Thou shalt not forswear (perjure) thyself, but shalt perform unto the Lord thine oaths:

But I say unto you, Swear not at all; neither by heaven; for it is God's throne:

Nor by the earth; for it is his footstool: neither by Jerusalem; for it is the city of the great King.

Neither shalt thou swear by thy head, because thou canst not make one hair white or black.

But let your communication be, Yea, yea; Nay, nay (Yes, yes; No, no): for whatsoever is more than these cometh of (comes from) evil .

Ye have heard that it hath been said, An eye for an eye, and a tooth for a tooth:

The Sermon On The Mount continued:

But I say unto you, That ye resist not evil: but whosoever shall smite (slap) thee on thy right cheek, turn to him the other also.

And if any man will sue thee at the law, and take away thy coat, let him have thy cloak also.

And whosoever shall compel thee to go a mile, go with him twain (two).

Give to him that asketh thee, and from him that would borrow of thee turn not thou away.

Ye have heard that it hath been said, Thou shalt love thy neighbour, and hate thine enemy.

But I say unto you, Love your enemies, bless them that curse you, do good to them that hate you, and pray for them which despitefully use you, and persecute you;

The Sermon On The Mount continued:

That ye may be the children of your Father which is in heaven: for he maketh his sun to rise on the evil and on the good, and sendeth rain on the just and on the unjust.

For if ye love them which love you, what reward have ye? do not even the publicans (tax collectors) the same?

And if ye salute your brethren only, what do ye more than others? do not even the publicans so?

Be ye therefore perfect, even as your Father which is in heaven is perfect.   (Matthew 5:1-48)

Take heed that ye do not your alms (charity) before men, to be seen of them: otherwise ye have no reward of your Father which is in heaven.

The Sermon On The Mount continued:

Therefore when thou doest thine alms, do not sound a trumpet before thee, as the hypocrites do... in the streets, that they may have glory of men. Verily I say unto you, They have their reward.

But when thou doest alms, let not thy left hand know what thy right hand doeth:

That thine alms may be in secret: and thy Father which seeth in secret himself shall reward thee openly.

And when thou prayest, thou shalt not be as the hypocrites are: for they love to pray standing in ... the corners of the streets, that they may be seen of men. Verily I say unto you, They have their reward.

But thou, when thou prayest, enter into thy closet, and when thou hast

The Sermon On The Mount continued:

shut thy door, pray to thy Father which is in secret; and thy Father which seeth in secret shall reward thee openly.

But when ye pray, use not vain repetitions, as the heathen do: for they think that they shall be heard for their much speaking.

Be not ye therefore like unto them: for your Father knoweth what things ye have need of, before ye ask him.

Do Your Alms In Secret, And Your Father Shall Reward You Openly.

The Sermon On The Mount continued:

After this manner therefore pray ye:

Our Father which art in heaven, Hallowed (Honored, Holy) be thy name.

Thy kingdom come. Thy will be done in earth, as it is in heaven.

Give us this day our daily bread.

And forgive us our debts, as we forgive our debtors.*

And lead us not into temptation, but deliver us from evil: For thine is the kingdom, and the power, and the glory, for ever. Amen.

*(alternative translation) And forgive us our trespasses, as we also forgive those who trespass against us.

For if ye forgive men their trespasses (debts), your heavenly Father will also forgive you:

The Sermon On The Mount continued:

But if ye forgive not men their trespasses, neither will your Father forgive your trespasses.

Moreover when ye fast, be not, as the hypocrites, of a sad countenance: for they disfigure their faces, that they may appear unto men to fast. Verily I say unto you, They have their reward.

But thou, when thou fastest, anoint thine head, and wash thy face;

That thou appear not unto men to fast, but unto thy Father which is in secret: and thy Father, which seeth in secret, shall reward thee openly.

Lay not up for yourselves treasures upon earth, where moth and rust doth corrupt, and where thieves break through and steal:

But lay up for yourselves treasures in heaven, where neither moth nor

The Sermon On The Mount continued:

rust doth corrupt, and where thieves do not break through nor steal:

For where your treasure is, there will your heart be also.

The light of the body is the eye: if therefore thine eye be single (sound), thy whole body shall be full of light.

But if thine eye be evil, thy whole body shall be full of darkness. If therefore the light that is in thee be darkness, how great is that darkness!

No man can serve two masters: for either he will hate the one, and love the other; or else he will hold to the one, and despise the other. Ye cannot serve God and mammon (money).

Therefore I say unto you, Take no thought for your life, what ye shall eat, or what ye shall drink; nor yet for your body, what ye shall put on. Is not the

The Sermon On The Mount continued:
life more than meat, and the body than raiment (clothing).

Behold the fowls (birds) of the air: for they sow not, neither do they reap, nor gather into barns; yet your heavenly Father feedeth them. Are ye not much better than they?

Which of you by taking thought can add one cubit* unto his stature?

And why take ye thought for raiment? Consider the lilies of the field, how they grow; they toil not, neither do they spin:

And yet I say unto you, That even Solomon in all his glory was not arrayed like one of these.

Wherefore, if God so clothe the grass of the field, which to day is, and to morrow is cast into the oven, shall he not much more clothe you, O ye of little faith?   *(about eighteen inches)

The Sermon On The Mount continued:

Therefore take no thought, saying, What shall we eat? or, What shall we drink? or, Wherewithal shall we be clothed?

For your heavenly Father knoweth that ye have need of all these things.

But seek ye first the kingdom of God, and his righteousness; and all these things shall be added unto you.

Take therefore no thought for the morrow: for the morrow shall take thought for the things of itself. Sufficient unto the day is the evil (trouble) thereof. (Matthew 6:1-34)

Judge not, that ye be not judged.

For with what judgment ye judge, ye shall be judged: and with what measure ye mete (distribute), it shall be measured to you again.

The Sermon On The Mount continued:

And why beholdest thou the mote (twig) that is in thy brother's eye, but considerest not the beam that is in thine own eye?

Or how wilt thou say to thy brother, Let me pull out the mote out of thine eye; and, behold, a beam is in thine own eye?

Thou hypocrite, first cast out the beam out of thine own eye; and then shalt thou see clearly to cast out the mote out of thy brother's eye.

Give not that which is holy unto the dogs, neither cast ye your pearls before swine, lest they trample them under their feet, and turn again and rend (attack) you.

Ask, and it shall be given you; seek, and ye shall find; knock, and it shall be opened unto you:

The Sermon On The Mount continued:

For every one that asketh receiveth; and he that seeketh findeth; and to him that knocketh it shall be opened.

Or what man is there of you, whom if his son ask bread, will he give him a stone?

Or if he ask a fish, will he give him a serpent?

If ye then, being evil, know how to give good gifts unto your children, how much more shall your Father which is in heaven give good things to them that ask him?

Therefore all things whatsoever ye would that men should do to you, do ye even so to them: for this is the law and the prophets.

Enter ye in at the strait (narrow) gate: for wide is the gate, and broad is

The Sermon On The Mount continued:

the way, that leadeth to destruction, and many there be which go in thereat:

Because strait is the gate, and narrow is the way, which leadeth unto life, and few there be that find it.

Beware of false prophets, which come to you in sheep's clothing, but inwardly they are ravening wolves.

Ye shall know them by their fruits. Do men gather grapes of thorns, or figs of thistles?

Even so every good tree bringeth forth good fruit; but a corrupt tree bringeth forth evil fruit.

A good tree cannot bring forth evil fruit, neither can a corrupt tree bring forth good fruit.

Every tree that bringeth not forth good fruit is hewn (cut) down, and cast into the fire.

The Sermon On The Mount continued:

Wherefore (thus) by their fruits ye shall know them.

Not every one that saith unto me, Lord, Lord, shall enter into the kingdom of heaven; but he that doeth the will of my Father which is in heaven.

Many will say to me in that day, Lord, Lord, have we not prophesied in thy name? and in thy name have cast out devils? and in thy name done many wonderful works?

And then will I profess (declare) unto them, I never knew you: depart from me, ye that work iniquity.

Therefore whosoever heareth these sayings of mine, and doeth them, I will liken him unto a wise man, which built his house upon a rock:

And the rain descended, and the floods came, and the winds blew, and

The Sermon On The Mount continued:

beat upon that house; and it fell not: for it was founded upon a rock.

And every one that heareth these sayings of mine, and doeth them not, shall be likened unto a foolish man, which built his house upon the sand:

And the rain descended, and the floods came, and the winds blew, and beat upon that house; and it fell: and great was the fall of it.

And it came to pass, when Jesus had ended these sayings, the people were astonished at his doctrine:

For he taught them as one having authority, and not as the scribes. (Matthew 7:1-29)

He That Doeth The Will Of My Father Shall Enter Into The Kingdom Of Heaven.

Serving God

No servant can serve two masters: for either he will hate the one, and love the other; or else he will hold to the one, and despise the other. Ye cannot serve God and mammon (money).
(Luke 16:13)

By this shall all men know that ye are my disciples, if ye have love one to another. (John 13:35)

As we have therefore opportunity, let us do good unto all men, especially unto them who are of the household of faith. (Galatians 6:10)

Serving Others

He that is greatest among you shall be your servant.

And whosoever shall exalt himself shall be abased (humbled); and he that shall humble himself shall be exalted. (Matthew 23:11-12)

Shame

If any man suffer as a Christian, let him not be ashamed; but let him glorify God on this behalf.
(1 Peter 4:16)

Sickness

When Jesus departed thence, two blind men followed him, crying, and saying, Thou son of David, have mercy on us.

And when he was come into the house, the blind men came to him: and Jesus saith unto them, Believe ye that I am able to do this? They said unto him, Yea, Lord.

Then touched he their eyes, saying, According to your faith be it unto you.

And their eyes were opened (restored to sight). (Matthew 9:27-30)

Signs Of The End Of Time

Please see **End**.

Sin

She shall bring forth a son, and thou shalt call his name Jesus: for he shall save his people from their sins. (Matthew 1:21)

I came not to call the righteous, but sinners to repentance. (Luke 5:32)

But God commendeth his love toward us, in that, while we were yet sinners, Christ died for us. (Romans 5:8)

For the wages of sin is death; but the gift of God is eternal life through Jesus Christ our Lord. (Romans 6:23)

There hath no temptation taken you (have not been tempted) but such as is common to man: God is faithful,

who will not suffer (allow) you to be tempted above that ye are able (to resist); but will with the temptation also make a way to escape, that ye may be able to bear (resist) it.
(1 Corinthians 10:13)

Draw nigh to God, and he will draw nigh to you. Cleanse your hands, ye sinners; and purify your hearts, ye double minded. (James 4:8)

Soul

What shall it profit a man, if he shall gain the whole world, and lose his own soul? (Mark 8:36)

He that cometh from above is above all: he that is of the earth is earthly, and speaketh of the earth: he that cometh from heaven is above all.
(John 3:31)

Sower

He spake (spoke) many things unto them in parables, saying, Behold, a sower went forth to sow (plant);

And when he sowed, some seeds fell by the way side, and the fowls came and devoured them up:

Some fell upon stony places,...

And when the sun was up, they were scorched; ..

And some fell among thorns; and the thorns sprung up, and choked them:

But other fell into good ground, and brought forth fruit, some an hundredfold, some sixtyfold, some thirtyfold.   (Matthew 13:3-8)

Hear ye therefore the parable of the sower.

He that received seed into the good ground is he that heareth the word, and understandeth it; which also beareth fruit, and bringeth forth, some an hundredfold, some sixty, some thirty. (Matthew 13:18-23)

Speaking Badly (Maliciously)

If any man among you seem to be religious, and bridleth (controls) not his tongue, but deceiveth his own heart, this man's religion is vain. (James 1:26)

Let no corrupt communication proceed out of your mouth, but that which is good to the use of edifying, that it may minister (furnish) grace unto the hearers. (Ephesians 4:29)

For he that will love life, and see good days, let him refrain his tongue from evil, and his lips that they speak no guile: (1 Peter 3:10)

Spirit

The fruit (product) of the Spirit is love, joy, peace, longsuffering, gentleness, goodness, faith. (Galatians 5:22)

Also see **Holy Spirit**

Spirit Of Truth
Please see **Honesty**

Spirituality

Follow peace with all men, and holiness, without which no man shall see the Lord: (Hebrews 12:14)

Spiritual Health

Christ also suffered for us, leaving us an example, that ye should follow his steps:

Who his own self (Jesus) bare our sins in his own body on the tree (cross), that we, being dead to sins, should live unto righteousness: by whose (Jesus') stripes (wounds) ye were healed.
(1 Peter 2:21,24)

Spiritual Trials

Blessed is the man that endureth (resists) temptation: for when he is tried, he shall receive the crown of life, which the Lord hath promised to them that love him. (James 1:12)

Please see **Temptation**.

Strangers

Be not forgetful to entertain strangers: for thereby some have entertained angels unawares. (Hebrews 13:2)

Strength

He said unto me, My grace is sufficient for thee: for my strength is made perfect in (your) weakness.

Most gladly therefore will I rather glory in my infirmities, that the power of Christ may rest upon me.
(2 Corinthians 12:9)

Finally, my brethren, be strong in the Lord, and in the power of his might.
(Ephesians 6:10)

I can do all things through Christ which strengtheneth me.
(Philippians 4:13)

Stress, Coping With It

Let not your heart be troubled: ye believe in God, believe also in me.
(John 14:1)

Believest thou not (Don't you believe) that I am in the Father, and the Father in me?..I speak not of myself: but the Father that dwelleth in me, he doeth the works.

If ye shall ask any thing in my name, I will do it.

And I will pray the Father, and he shall give you another Comforter, that he may abide with you for ever;

I will not leave you comfortless: I will come to you.

But the Comforter, which is the Holy Ghost, whom the Father will send in my name, he shall teach you all things, and bring all things to your remembrance, whatsoever I have said unto you.

Peace I leave with you, my peace I give unto you: not as the world giveth, give I unto you. Let not your heart be troubled, neither let it be afraid.
(John 14:10,14,18,26-27)

Suffering

We are troubled on every side, yet not distressed; we are perplexed, but not in despair;

For our light affliction, which is but for a moment, worketh for us a far more exceeding and eternal weight of glory;

While we look not at the things which are seen, but at the things which are not seen: for the things which are seen are temporal; but the things which are not seen are eternal.
(2 Corinthians 4:8,17-18)

We Are Troubled, But Not In Despair.

Forasmuch then as (seeing that) Christ hath suffered for us in the flesh, arm yourselves likewise with the same mind: for he that hath suffered in the flesh (body) hath ceased from sin;

That he no longer should live the rest of his time in the flesh to the lusts of men, but to the will of God.
(1 Peter 4:1-2)

No Longer Live To The Lusts Of Men, But To The Will Of God.

Tears Wiped Away

I saw a new heaven and a new earth: for the first heaven and the first earth were passed away; and there was no more sea.

And God shall wipe away all tears from their eyes; and there shall be no more death, neither sorrow, nor crying, neither shall there be any more pain: for the former things are passed away. (Revelation 21:1,4)

God Shall Wipe Away All Tears.

Temptation

When the tempter (Satan) came to him, he said, If thou be the Son of God, command that these stones be made bread.

Jesus said unto him, It is written again, Thou shalt not tempt the Lord thy God. (Matthew 4:3,7)

And he came out, and went, as he was wont (accustomed), to the mount of Olives; and his disciples also followed him.

And when he was at the place, he said unto them, Pray that ye enter not into temptation. (Luke 22:39-40)

Let no man say when he is tempted, I am tempted of God: for God cannot be tempted with evil, neither tempteth he any man: (James 1:12-13)

Also see **Spiritual Trials**.

The Last Supper

Being now justified (cleansed) by his blood, we shall be saved.

By Leonardo Da Vinci 1452-1519

Thirst

Please see **Hunger**.

Tidings Of Great Joy

The angel said unto them, Fear not: for, behold, I bring you good tidings of great joy, which shall be to all people.

For unto you is born this day in the city of David a Saviour, which is Christ the Lord.   (Luke 2:10-11)

Trinity, Holy

There are three that bear record in heaven, the Father, the Word, and the Holy Ghost: and these three are one. (1 John 5:7)

Trouble
See **God's Help In Trouble.**

Trust In God

We know that all things work together for good to them that love God, to them who are the called according to his purpose. (Romans 8:28)

But we had the sentence of death in ourselves, that we should not trust in ourselves, but in God which raiseth the dead:

Who delivered us from so great a death,..in whom we trust that he will yet deliver us; (2 Corinthians 1:9-10)

Humble yourselves therefore under the mighty hand of God, that he may exalt you in due time:

Casting all your care upon him; for he careth for you. (1 Peter 5:6-7)

Understanding

If any of you lack wisdom, let him ask of God, that giveth to all men liberally, and upbraideth (blames) not; and it shall be given him. (James 1:5)

Vengeance

Dearly beloved, avenge not yourselves, but rather give place unto wrath (anger): for it is written, Vengeance is mine; I will repay, saith the Lord.

Therefore if thine enemy hunger, feed him; if he thirst, give him drink: for in so doing thou shalt heap coals of fire on his head.   (Romans 12:19-20)

Vengeance Is Mine..
Saith The Lord.

Wait On The Lord

Wait for his Son from heaven, whom he raised from the dead, even Jesus, which delivered us from the wrath (anger or punishment) to come.
(1 Thessalonians 1:10)

Let us hold fast the profession of our faith without wavering; (for he is faithful that promised;) (Hebrews 10:23)

Walk In The Light

Jesus saith unto him, I am the way, the truth, and the life: no man cometh unto the Father, but by me.
(John 14:6)

But if we walk in the light, as he is in the light, we have fellowship one with another, and the blood of Jesus Christ his Son cleanseth us from all sin.
(1 John 1:7)

Wisdom

God, who commanded the light to shine out of darkness, hath shined in our hearts, to give the light of the knowledge of the glory of God in the face of Jesus Christ. (2 Corinthians 4:6)

Humble yourselves therefore under the mighty hand of God, that he may exalt you in due time:

Casting all your care upon him; for he careth for you. (1 Peter 5:6-7)

Please see **Understanding**.

Witness

Ye are the light of the world. A city that is set on an hill cannot be hid.

Neither do men light a candle, and put it under a bushel, but on a candlestick; and it giveth light unto all that are in the house.

Let your light so shine before men, that they may see your good works, and glorify your Father which is in heaven.   (Matthew 5:14-16)

Also I say unto you, Whosoever shall confess (acknowledge) me before men, him shall the Son of man also confess before the angels of God:
(Luke 12:8)

I will give you a mouth and wisdom, which all your adversaries shall not be able to gainsay (deny) nor resist.
(Luke 21:15)

Let Your Light Shine Before Men.

Word Of God

It is written, Man shall not live by bread alone, but by every word that proceedeth out of the mouth of God. (Matthew 4:4)

Blessed are they that hear the word of God, and keep it. (Luke 11:28)

Heaven and earth shall pass away: but my words shall not pass away. (Luke 21:33)

Then said Jesus to those Jews which believed on him, If ye continue in my word, then are ye my disciples indeed; (John 8:31)

Faith cometh by hearing, and hearing by the word of God. (Romans 10:17)

As newborn babes, desire the sincere milk (nourishment) of the word , that ye may grow thereby: (1 Peter 2:2)

He received from God the Father honour and glory, when there came such a voice to him from the excellent glory, This is my beloved Son, in whom I am well pleased. (2 Peter 1:17)

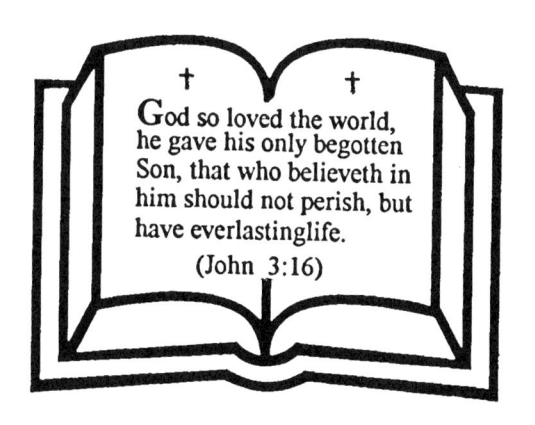

> God so loved the world, he gave his only begotten Son, that who believeth in him should not perish, but have everlasting life.
> (John 3:16)

Worldliness

For what is a man advantaged, if he gain the whole world, and lose himself, or be cast away? (Luke 9:25)

Epilogue
New Testament Selections

As the lightning (sun, sunrise) cometh out of the east, and shineth even unto the west; so shall also the coming of the Son of man be.

Immediately after the tribulation of those days shall the sun be darkened, and the moon shall not give her light, and the stars shall fall from heaven, and the powers of the heavens shall be shaken:

And then shall appear the sign of the Son of man in heaven: and then shall all the tribes of the earth mourn, and they shall see the Son of man coming in the clouds of heaven with power and great glory.

And he shall send his angels with a great sound of a trumpet, and they shall gather together his elect from the four winds, from one end of heaven to the other.

Heaven and earth shall pass away, but my words shall not pass away.

Watch therefore: for ye know not what hour your Lord doth come.

Therefore be ye also ready: for in such an hour as ye think not the Son of man cometh.

Blessed is that servant, whom his lord when he cometh shall find so doing (looking for the Lord).
(Matthew 24:27,29-31,35,42,44,46)

My Words Shall Not Pass Away.

When the Son of man shall come in his glory, and all the holy angels with him, then shall he sit upon the throne of his glory:

And before him shall be gathered all nations: and he shall separate them one from another, as a shepherd divideth his sheep from the goats:

And he shall set the sheep on his right hand, but the goats on the left.

Then shall the King say unto them on his right hand, Come, ye blessed of my Father, inherit the kingdom prepared for you from the foundation of the world: (Matthew 25:14,31-34)

End Of
New Testament Section

Notes

Selections from the Psalms, Proverbs and the Ten Commandments of the Old Testament

Torah

תורה

The Old Testament

The Bible of the Hebrews was written over a period of more than 500 years. Essentially religious, the Old Testament is also strongly historical and contains laws and urgings.

The main subjects are the unique glory of God (Yahweh), the Covenants He made with Israel through Noah, Abraham, Moses, and according to the Judeans also through King David.

The Law, God's revelation through the prophets, the nature of humanity, sin and redemption, and the right worship of Yahweh are likewise important.

The Hebrews believed that their religion was founded on covenants (promises) that God offered, to make them his chosen people and to protect them, if they obeyed his statutes.

Israel was prohibited from worshipping any other god. Yahweh was supreme over everything. The Hebrews were to be a holy people, separated from all corruption.

Many laws are in the Pentateuch, or Torah, the first five books. Among the unique commandments, the most important are the Ten Commandments.

The Torah (Law) was the comprehensive religious and civil law for the whole nation, with the emphasis on righteousness. Yahweh being a just God, all wrong doing was offensive to him. Forgiveness followed sincere repentance.

Ten Commandments

A group of godly laws contained in the Bible, the Ten Commandments constitute the basic moral rules of Judaism and Christianity. The holy scriptures state that God presented the commandments inscribed on two stone tablets to Moses, on Mount Sinai. The beginning commandments are about honoring one God, who tolerates no others or the making and worship of graven images, prohibits taking God's name in vain, and insists on keeping holy the Sabbath. Then occur the commandments controlling the conduct of humans with one another and honoring one's parents. These are followed by forbidding killing, adultery, stealing, false witness, and coveting.

TEN COMMANDMENTS

1) Thou shalt have no other gods before me.

2) Thou shalt not make unto thee any graven image...Thou shalt not bow down thyself to them, nor serve them...

3) Thou shalt not take the name of the Lord thy God in vain;

4) Remember the sabbath day, to keep it holy.

5) Honour thy father and thy mother: that thy days may be long upon the land which the Lord thy God giveth thee.

6) Thou shalt not kill.

7) Thou shalt not commit adultery.

8) Thou shalt not steal.

9) Thou shalt not bear false witness against thy neighbour.

10) Thou shalt not covet thy neighbour's house, thou shalt not covet thy neighbour's wife, nor any thing that is thy neighbour's.

(Exodus 20:3-17)

Topical Contents And Index
Old Testament Section

Abominations	226
Abundance	204
Acknowledge Him	226
Anger	205, 226
Charity	227
Comfort In Trouble & Fear	205
Contentment	206
Courage	206
Dealing With Enemies	227
Death	206
Discretion	228
Enemies	207
Epilogue Old Testament	235
Eternal Life	207

Fear	208
Fear Of The Lord	228
Fool	228
Guiding Your Paths	229
Healing	229
Help	209
Hope	209
Joy	210, 230
Kingship Of God (Yahweh)	210
Long Life	211, 230
Lust	231
Loving The Lord	212
Lying	212
Meekness	212
Medicine	231
Mercy	213
Money	213, 231
Name Of God	214

Obedience	232
Old Age	214
Parental Obligations	232
Path Of Life	215
Patience	232
Peace, Shalom	216
Praise The Lord	217
Pride	232
Protection By The Lord	217
Rejoice	218
Resting In The Lord	218
Revenge	219
Righteousness	233
Salvation	219
Self-Righteousness	233
Sickness	220
Speaking	233
Strength	220
Stress	221

Teach Me, O Lord	221
The Ten Commandments	197, 198
Trust In The Lord	222
Understanding	222
Wait On The Lord	223, 233
Wisdom	234
Word Of God	223, 234

Psalms

These beautiful and inspiring Hebrew religious poems constitute one of the best known books of the Bible. The psalms are similar to hymns. They have been regarded as the most refined and clear collection of writings about the deeper life of mankind, including man's meditations, yearnings and devotions to God.

One of the best loved psalms is *"The Lord is my shepherd.... Surely goodness and mercy shall follow me all the days of my life: and I will dwell in the house of the Lord for ever."*
(Psalms 23:1-6)

There is no aspect of man's thoughts, religious experiences, or needs that is not discussed in the psalms.

Abundance

A Psalm of David. The earth is the Lord's, and the fulness thereof; the world, and they that dwell therein.

For he hath founded it upon the seas, and established it upon the floods.

Who shall ascend into the hill of the Lord? or who shall stand in his holy place?

He that hath clean hands, and a pure heart; who hath not lifted up his soul unto vanity, nor sworn deceitfully.

He shall receive the blessing from the Lord, and righteousness from the God of his salvation. (Psalms 24:1-5)

The Earth Is The Lord's, And The Fulness Thereof.

O fear the Lord, ye his saints: for there is no want to them that fear him.
The young lions do lack, and suffer hunger: but they that seek the Lord shall not want any good thing.
(Psalms 34:9, 10)

Anger

His anger endureth but a moment; in his favour is life: weeping may endure for a night, but joy cometh in the morning. (Psalms 30:5)

Comfort In Trouble And Fear

God is our refuge and strength, a very present help in trouble.
Therefore will not we fear, though the earth be removed, and though the mountains be carried into the midst of the sea; (Psalms 46:1-2)

Contentment

He that dwelleth in the secret place of the most High shall abide under the shadow of the Almighty.

I will say of the Lord, He is my refuge and my fortress: my God; in him will I trust.   (Psalms 91:1-2)

Courage

Wait on the Lord: be of good courage, and he shall strengthen thine heart: wait, I say, on the Lord. (Psalms 27:14)

Death

God will redeem my soul from the power of the grave: for he shall receive me. (Psalms 49:15)

Enemies

I will call upon the Lord, who is worthy to be praised: so shall I be saved from mine enemies. (Psalms 18:3)

For in the time of trouble he shall hide me in his pavilion (shelter): in the secret of his tabernacle (temple) shall he hide me; he shall set me up upon a rock.

And now shall mine head be lifted up above mine enemies round about me: therefore will I offer in his tabernacle sacrifices of joy; I will sing, yea, I will sing praises unto the Lord.
(Psalms 27:5-6)

Eternal Life

God will redeem my soul from the power of the grave: for he shall receive me. (Psalms 49:15)

Thou, which hast showed me great and sore troubles, shalt quicken me again, and shalt bring me up again from the depths of the earth.
(Psalms 71:20)

Fear

God is our refuge and strength, a very present help in trouble.
(Psalms 46:1)

He shall cover thee with his feathers, and under his wings shalt thou trust: his truth shall be thy shield and buckler.

Thou shalt not be afraid for the terror by night; nor for the arrow that flieth by day;

Nor for the pestilence (epidemic) that walketh in darkness; nor for the destruction that wasteth at noonday.
(Psalms 91:4-6)

Help

I will lift up mine eyes unto the hills, from whence cometh my help.

My help cometh from the Lord, which made heaven and earth.
(Psalms 121:1-2)

Hope

Wait on the Lord: be of good courage, and he shall strengthen thine heart: wait, I say, on the Lord.
(Psalms 27:14)

Behold, the eye of the Lord is upon them that fear him, upon them that hope in his mercy;

To deliver their soul from death, and to keep them alive in famine.
(Psalms 33:18-19)

Joy

The pastures are clothed with flocks; the valleys also are covered over with corn; they shout for joy, they also sing.   (Psalms 65:13)

Make a joyful noise unto God, all ye lands:
Sing forth the honour of his name: make his praise glorious.
(Psalms 66:1-2)

Kingship Of God

Great is the Lord, and greatly to be praised; and his greatness is unsearchable.
One generation shall praise thy works to another, and shall declare thy mighty acts. (Psalms 145:3-4)

Thy kingdom is an everlasting kingdom, and thy dominion endureth throughout all generations.
(Psalms 145:13)

Long Life

Because he hath set his love upon me, therefore will I deliver him: I will set him on high, because he hath known my name.

He shall call upon me, and I will answer him: I will be with him in trouble; I will deliver him, and honour him.

With long life will I satisfy him, and show him my salvation.
(Psalms 91:14-16)

Make A Joyful Noise Unto God.

Loving The Lord

I love the Lord, because he hath heard my voice and my supplications.

Because he hath inclined his ear unto me, therefore will I call upon him as long as I live. (Psalms 116:1-2)

Lying

I hate and abhor lying: but thy law do I love. (Psalms 119:163)

Meekness

The meek will he guide in judgment: and the meek will he teach his way. (Psalms 25:9)

For the Lord taketh pleasure in his people: he will beautify the meek (humble) with salvation. (Psalms 149:4)

Mercy

Behold, the eye of the Lord is upon them that fear him, upon them that hope in his mercy;

To deliver their soul from death, and to keep them alive in famine.
(Psalms 33:18-19)

The mercy of the Lord is from everlasting to everlasting upon them that fear him, and his righteousness unto children's children;

To such as keep his covenant, and to those that remember his commandments to do them.
(Psalms 103:17-18)

Money

A little that a righteous man hath is better than the riches of many wicked.
(Psalms 37:16)

Name of God

I will praise the name of God with a song, and will magnify him with thanksgiving.   (Psalms 69:30)

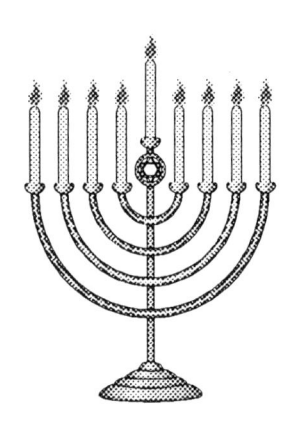

Old Age

Cast me not off in the time of old age; forsake me not when my strength faileth.

O God, be not far from me: O my God, make haste for my help.
(Psalms 71:9,12)

Thou shalt guide me with thy counsel, and afterward receive me to glory.

Whom have I in heaven but thee? and there is none upon earth that I desire beside thee.

My flesh and my heart faileth: but God is the strength of my heart, and my portion for ever. (Psalms 73:24-26)

Thou Shalt Guide Me And Afterward Receive Me To Glory.

Path Of Life

Thou wilt show me the path of life: in thy presence is fulness of joy; at thy right hand there are pleasures for evermore. (Psalms 1:11)

Peace, Shalom, שלום

The Lord is my shepherd; I shall not want.

He maketh me to lie down in green pastures: he leadeth me beside the still waters.

He restoreth my soul: he leadeth me in the paths of righteousness for his name's sake.

Yea, though I walk through the valley of the shadow of death, I will fear no evil: for thou art with me; thy rod and thy staff they comfort me.

Thou preparest a table before me in the presence of mine enemies: thou anointest my head with oil; my cup runneth over.

Surely goodness and mercy shall follow me all the days of my life: and I will dwell in the house of the Lord for ever.   (Psalms 23:1-6)

Praise The Lord

My mouth shall speak the praise of the Lord: and let all flesh (people) bless his holy name for ever and ever. (Psalms 145:21)

Praise ye the Lord. Praise the Lord, O my soul.
While I live will I praise the Lord: I will sing praises unto my God while I have any being. (Psalms 146:1-2)

Protection By The Lord

The Lord is my light and my salvation; whom shall I fear? the Lord is the strength of my life; of whom shall I be afraid? (Psalms 27:1)

The Lord preserveth all them that love him: but all the wicked will he destroy. (Psalms 145:20)

Rejoice

Be glad in the Lord, and rejoice, ye righteous: and shout for joy, all ye that are upright in heart.
(Psalms 32:11)

Rejoice in the Lord, O ye righteous: for praise is comely (befitting) for the upright.   (Psalms 33:1)

This is the day which the Lord hath made; we will rejoice and be glad in it.   (Psalms 118:24)

Rejoice, O Ye Righteous!

Resting In The Lord

Cast thy burden upon the Lord, and he shall sustain thee: he shall never suffer the righteous to be moved.
(Psalms 55:22)

Revenge

The righteous shall rejoice when he seeth the vengeance..in (on) the wicked. (Psalms 58:10)

O Lord God, to whom vengeance belongeth; O God, to whom vengeance belongeth, show thyself. (Psalms 94:1)

Thou wast a God that forgavest them, though thou tookest vengeance of their inventions (transgressions). (Psalms 99:8)

Salvation

The salvation of the righteous is of the Lord: he is their strength in the time of trouble.

And the Lord shall help them, and deliver them: he shall deliver them from the wicked, and save them, because they trust in him. (Psalms 37:39-40)

Sickness

Yea, though I walk through the valley of the shadow of death, I will fear no evil: for thou art with me; thy rod and thy staff they comfort me.
(Psalms 23:4)

The Salvation Of The Righteous Is Of The Lord.

Strength

I will lift up mine eyes unto the hills, from whence cometh my help.

My help cometh from the Lord, which made heaven and earth.
(Psalms 121:1-2)

Stress

Thou shalt not be afraid for the terror by night; nor for the arrow that flieth by day;

Nor for the pestilence (epidemic) that walketh in darkness; nor for the destruction that wasteth at noonday. (Psalms 91:5-6)

Then they cried unto the Lord in their trouble, and he delivered them out of their distresses. (Psalms 107:6)

Teach Me, O Lord
Please see the **Word of God**

Thou Shalt Not Be Afraid.

Trust In The Lord My Rock

The Lord is my rock, and my fortress, and my deliverer; my God, my strength, in whom I will trust; my buckler, and the horn of my salvation, and my high tower. (Psalms 18:2)

The Lord redeemeth (saves) the soul of his servants: and none of them that trust in him shall be desolate. (Psalms 34:22)

I will say of the Lord, He is my refuge and my fortress: my God; in him will I trust. (Psalms 91:2)

Understanding, Receiving It

The fear of the Lord is the beginning of wisdom: a good understanding have all they that do his commandments: his praise endureth for ever. (Psalms 111:10)

WAIT ON THE LORD

Wait on the Lord: be of good courage, and he shall strengthen thine heart: wait, I say, on the Lord.
(Psalms 27:14)

BE OF GOOD COURAGE.

WORD OF GOD

Teach me, O Lord,

Make me to go in the path of thy commandments...

How sweet are thy words...

Thy word is a lamp unto my feet, and a light unto my path.

Hold me up, and I shall be safe: and I will respect thy statutes.
(from Psalms 119:33-117)

Notes

Proverbs

The uplifting Book of Proverbs is a collection of sacred and virtuous teachings and wise customs. These have been taught to young Jews by their wise men ever since the exile of the Jews in Babylonia (597-538 B.C.).

The predominant idea of Proverbs is wisdom, not merely knowing a lot of things, but also knowing and doing the right thing.

Some parts of proverbs speak warnings; other parts offer short sayings or aphorisms obtained from experience.

These were presented so that people may have wisdom and understanding, as well as learn and follow the ways of righteous living. *Every word of God is pure: he is a shield unto them that put their trust in him.* (Proverbs 30:5)

Abominations

He that justifieth the wicked, and he that condemneth the just, even they both are abomination (utter disgust) to the Lord.   (Proverbs 17:15)

Acknowledge Him

Please see **Guiding your Paths.**

Anger

He that is slow to anger is better than the mighty; and he that ruleth his spirit than he that taketh a city. (Proverbs 16:32)

In All Thy Ways Acknowledge Him.

Charity

If thine enemy be hungry, give him bread to eat; and if he be thirsty, give him water to drink.

For thou shalt heap coals of fire upon his head (make him ashamed), and the Lord shall reward thee.
(Proverbs 25:21-22)

He That Is Slow To Anger Is Better Than The Mighty.

Dealing With Enemies
See **Enemies** in **Psalms**.

Discretion

He that keepeth his mouth keepeth his life: but he that openeth wide his lips shall have destruction.
(Proverbs 13:3)

The discretion of a man deferreth his anger; and it is his glory to pass over a transgression. (Proverbs 19:11)

Fear Of The Lord

The fear of the Lord is the beginning of wisdom: and the knowledge of the holy is understanding.
(Proverbs 9:10)

Fool

Wisdom is before him that hath understanding; but the eyes of a fool are in the ends of the earth (to no avail).

A foolish son is a grief to his father, and bitterness to her that bare him.
(Proverbs 17:24-25)

Guiding Your Paths

In all thy ways acknowledge him, and he shall direct thy paths.
(Proverbs 3:6)

Healing

My son, attend to my words; incline thine ear unto my sayings.

Let them not depart from thine eyes; keep them in the midst of thine heart.

For they are life unto those that find them, and health to all their flesh.
(Proverbs 4:20-22)

See also **Medicine** and **Wait On The Lord**.

Joy

Make A Joyful Noise Unto God.

Also see **Joy** in **Psalms** section.

Long Life

My son, forget not my law; but let thine heart keep my commandments:

For length of days, and long life, and peace, shall they add to thee. (Proverbs 3:1-2).

Lust

Lust not after her beauty in thine heart; neither let her take (seduce) thee with her eyelids. (Proverbs 6:25)

So he that goeth in to (commits adultery with) his neighbour's wife; whosoever toucheth her shall not be innocent. (Proverbs 6:29)

Medicine

A merry heart doeth good like a medicine: but a broken spirit drieth the bones. (Proverbs 17:22)

Money

Whoso mocketh the poor reproacheth his Maker: and he that is glad at calamities shall not be unpunished. (Proverbs 17:5)

Obedience
Please see
Ten Commandments

Parental Obligations
Train up a child in the way he should go: and when he is old, he will not depart from it. (Proverbs 22:6)

Patience
The discretion of a man deferreth (restrains) his anger; and it is his glory to pass over a transgression.
(Proverbs 19:11)

Pride
Pride goeth before destruction, and an haughty spirit before a fall. (Proverbs 16:18)

Righteousness

The Lord is far from the wicked: but he heareth the prayer of the righteous. (Proverbs 15:29)

Self-righteousness

Seest thou a man wise in his own conceit (a conceited man)? there is more hope of a fool than of him. (Proverbs 26:12)

Speaking

There is (he) that speaketh like the piercings of a sword: but the tongue of the wise is health. (Proverbs 12:18)

Wait On The Lord

Say not, I will recompense (avenge) evil; but wait on the Lord, and he shall save thee. (Proverbs 20:22)

Wisdom

The fear of the Lord is the beginning of knowledge: but fools despise wisdom and instruction.

My son, hear the instruction of thy father, and forsake (abandon) not the law of thy mother: (Proverbs 1:7-8)

Word Of God

Every word of God is pure: he is a shield unto them that put their trust in him. (Proverbs 30:5)

The Lord Heareth The Prayer Of The Righteous.

Epilogue
Old Testament Selections

Let the God of my salvation be exalted. (Psalms 18:46)

Make a joyful noise unto God, all ye lands:

Sing forth the honour of his name: make his praise glorious.
(Psalms 66:1-2)

I will praise the name of God.. and will magnify him with thanksgiving. (Psalms 69:30)

In all thy ways acknowledge him, and he shall direct thy paths.
(Proverbs 3:6)

A Merry Heart Doeth Good Like A Medicine.

*The Lord Is My Shepherd.
I Shall Not Want;
He Restoreth My Soul.*

**End Of Selections
From The Old Testament**

Information for ordering this book is available from:

EPS Excel Publishing Services
P.O. Box 86
Wilmette, IL 60091

Email: EPS EXC PS@aol.com
FAX 847-251-1582

Notes